HINTS TO SINGERS

by

LILLIAN NORDICA

Together with an account of Lillian Nordica's training
for the opera, as told in the letters of the singer
and her mother, Amanda Allen Norton

Edited and with an Introduction by

WILLIAM ARMSTRONG

DOVER PUBLICATIONS, INC.
Mineola, New York

Bibliographical Note

This Dover edition, first published in 1998, is a lightly modified but otherwise unabridged republication of *Lillian Nordica's Hints to Singers / Together With an Account of Lillian Nordica's Training for the Opera, as Told in the Letters of the Singer and Her Mother, Amanda Allen Norton / Transcribed by William Armstrong,* originally published by E. P. Dutton and Company, New York, 1923. The eight black-and-white photographs, originally distributed throughout the book, are now grouped between pp. 26 and 27. Picture identifications are slightly expanded in the illustration list, p. vi, and in the captions. The caption for Mme. Schumann Heink's letter, p. iii, is newly added.

International Standard Book Number: 0-486-40094-8

Manufactured in the United States of America
Dover Publications, Inc., 31 East 2nd Street, Mineola, N.Y. 11501

Oct. 14. 1922.

My dear good friend
Every word Lillian
Fordica says in the book is
gospel truth – This noble great
soul died too soon for all of
us. She was the greatest most
wonderful American Singer –
what a voice and what ambition.
I shall always worship the
memory of the Artist, the woman.
Ernestine Schumann Heink

A letter from Mme. Ernestine Schumann Heink (1861–1936),
written on her personal stationery, addressed to William Armstrong in 1922,
one year before the original publication of Lillian Norton's book.

CONTENTS

HINTS TO SINGERS
by Lillian Nordica

ILLUSTRATIONS

Seven photographs of Lillian Nordica
and one of her mother—her constant companion on tour—
appear between pages 26 and 27.

INTRODUCTION
by William Armstrong

*H*ints to Singers is not a technical book on singing, but a summary of many things which Madame Nordica, in the making of a great career, learned through experience, and which she felt had helped her far toward ultimate success.

Her aim was to condense in brief paragraphs a combined total of value to any engaging in the singing life, and she expressed the wish that her book might be published at a price placing it within the reach of all.

Beyond the worth of views which she proved sound by practical experience, there is another value in *Hints to Singers,* the insight given into her attitude toward the singing life and the splendid reverence in which she held her art. There is given, too, insight of quite another and a purely human kind, of which it is the sole personal record that she left.

The story of the book's delay is curious. More than twenty years ago, Madame Nordica conceived the idea of writing with my aid *Hints to Singers.* Her life then throughout the musical season was one of constant appearances in concert and opera; her weeks of rest in summer-time were few. Those weeks found me engaged in gathering literary material in Europe. At last we got together to put her plan into execution.

Much of the book she dictated to me as we sat and talked by the wayside during long walks in the Black Forest or tramped along the hard, white highway leading from Menschenschwand to St. Blasien. Afterward, in America, came hours at her country house at Ardsley-on-Hudson, when she scanned with me every word and sentence, which remained just as she desired them.

One autumn night a publisher, anxious to bring out the manuscript, journeyed with me to Ardsley. Arrangements progressed favorably until Madame Nordica received some bindings of his output. These, condemned on sight by her as inartistic, closed the incident. Following delay, the book was taken up. This time, one among those about her, one who had never written, suggested, instead, an undertaking along ambitious lines, ignoring the original plan that had so long inspired her. Uncertain of her powers in writing, doubt assailed her. Again delay. Tired of vacillation, and with much else in hand to do, I put the manuscript of the book in a trunk to be sent to storage. There it remained for fifteen years, perhaps longer.

Two years after Madame Nordica's sad death at Batavia in the Dutch East Indies on her projected singing tour around the world, I went one day in Boston to see her two sisters, Mrs. William F. Baldwin and Mrs. George A. Walker. We talked together of *Hints to Singers,* the sole written record of herself and of her art left behind by Madame Nordica, a book into which she had put so much thought, time, and enthusiasm. Her sisters' wish, which accorded with my own, was that it be published.

To make it a joint tribute on their part, Mrs. Baldwin offered me family letters to include, written from abroad during Madame Nordica's study period there. Inquiry in New York, on my return, proved that, while the World War lasted, prospect of publishing a musical book would be hopeless. Yet again delay.

During preparation for press of my book, *The Romantic World of Music,* published by Messrs. E. P. Dutton and Company, the manuscript of *Hints to Singers* was brought to the attention of Mr. John Macrae of that firm. He immediately accepted it for publication. Meanwhile, both Mrs. Baldwin and Mrs. Walker had passed into the great beyond. In accord with her mother's wishes, Mrs. Lillian B. Burnham, niece and namesake of Madame Nordica, placed at my disposal the proffered letters, written from abroad by the singer and her mother, who accompanied her, and giving intimate detail of her plan of study and early appearances.

The letters precede *Hints to Singers.* Thus a fuller degree of sympathetic understanding of the book itself is apt to be established. They contain much of value to singers, and make appropriate addition to that which follows. Indeed, no better glimpse than they afford could well be given of the making of a prima donna and all that it entails. Alone, in the aspect of struggle made by these two women against obstacles, not the least of which was slender means, they constitute a human document.

Mrs. Norton's letters take up her daughter's singing life in 1878, when she toured Europe with Gilmore's Band. There are but two brief letters by Lillian Norton, herself, in the collection written by her mother to members of the family, and preserved by them. This fact she explained to her husband, Mr. Edwin Norton, very early in their absence and in the following paragraph:

"Lilly has all and more than she can do, so you must not think it strange if she does not write. She does not write any letters at all, but leaves that to me."

Mrs. Norton's own letters contain minute detail as to the future Nordica's plan of ardent study in Paris and Milan; tell of her first venture in opera at the latter city, and her debut at Brescia; her early subsequent engagements at Genoa and Novara; and culminate with a description of her entrance upon a brilliant recognition as *prima donna* at the Imperial Italian Opera, St. Petersburg.

Madame Nordica's career carried her art to the opera houses of Italy, Russia, France, Great Britain, Germany and her own country. No other American has yet developed gifts equal to hers in sustaining the Isolde, the Brünnhilde of the *Ring*, the Kundry, the Donna Anna, and the Valentina, which marked the apex of her singing life.

In the early years of her appearances in opera, she sang Violetta in *Traviata*, Gilda in *Rigoletto*, Inez in *L'Africaine*, Lucia in *Lucia di Lammermoor*, Ophelia in *Hamlet*, the Queen of Night in Mozart's *Magic Flute*, and more besides, making her repertory an array of coloratura parts that alone would have constituted both established reputation and satisfying career, considering the stages upon which she sang them.

Emerging from these, logically, gradually, she was heard as Marguerite in *Faust*, as Eudoxia in *La Juive*, Juliet in *Roméo et Juliet*, Amelia in *Ballo in Maschera*, Sulamith in *Reine de Saba*, Leonora in *Il Trovatore*, Venus in *Tannhäuser*, Elsa in *Lohengrin*, and many other roles before she ventured upon those heroic Wagnerian ones which marked her glorious zenith.

In all, Madame Nordica's operatic repertory, in addition to soprano parts in oratorios, numbered thirty-four roles. These roles extended all the way from Filina in *Mignon* and Norina in *Don Pasquale* to Desdemona in *Otello* and Carmen; from the Princepessa and Alice in *Roberto Il Diavolo*, to the Susanna in *Nozze di Figaro* (in which Cherubino was one of her earliest essays), Selika in *L'Africaine* and the Aïda.

Her versatility was tremendous, founded upon growth made step by step; upon study that meant toil; upon a training equal to demands corresponding with the stage of voice development, so that the golden prime of this last was reached with her heroic undertakings in Wagner's music dramas.

Following her debut appearances in Italy, Madame Nordica sang at the Imperial Italian Opera, St. Petersburg; at the Paris Opéra; throughout the British Provinces, and in America, making her London debut at the Royal Opera, Covent Garden, in 1887. That same year she made her real American debut at the Metropolitan, New York, in a company assembled by Mr. Henry E. Abbey.

Thereafter, during twenty-two years, and with seldom interruption, she appeared in opera at the Metropolitan, sustaining her position gloriously alongside the de Reszkes, Melba, Plançon, Calvé, and Eames in the golden days of that institution. Succeeding this, she was engaged at the Manhattan Opera House for a brief period, prior to returning to her first love, the Metropolitan.

In the Covent Garden season, which followed the winter one at the Metropolitan, Madame Nordica sang often, and also in oratorio in the cathedral cities of England, establishing for herself a great international position. As Elsa, she sang in the Bayreuth production of *Lohengrin;* in the Munich Wagner Festivals she appeared as Brünnhilde of the *Ring* and as Isolde; this last role, in addition to the Elsa, she interpreted in French at the Paris Opéra, and, besides other Wagnerian performances in Germany, she sang at the Berlin Royal Opera.

In recurring years, Madame Nordica, on tour with the Metropolitan organization, sang in frequent seasons at Chicago, Boston, Philadelphia and elsewhere, appearing also as soloist in music festivals, in orchestral concerts and in numberless recitals. Few have inspired such warm appreciation so ardently displayed by audiences everywhere. This was not alone due to her art and golden voice, but to her personal, magnetic charm, her queenly figure, and her bearing, so grandly gracious. These left an impress that doubtless still lingers in the heart of many an American.

Always she was reaching out to new endeavor. After a career of thirty-six years this spirit led her to undertake in 1913 a concert tour around the world. Shipwrecked in the Gulf of Papua, she reached Australia, her destination, ill. Struggling against physical disability she sang. Then proceeded, still ill, on her projected journey. Wearily she reached the last objective in it granted her, Batavia in the Dutch East Indies. There she died in sad isolation, tended to the end by her staunchly faithful friend and accompanist, Romayne Simmons.

Lillian Nordica's Training for the Opera

As Told in the Letters of Amanda Allen Norton
(The Singer's Mother) and Lillian Nordica

To make more complete the chronicle of Lillian Norton's student years, it has seemed well to record certain incidents that she herself told me and which precede the period when her mother's letters took it up.

Of her childhood days in Boston as Lillian Norton, the great singer spoke of little things which showed that from the outset music had absorbed her life. Bribed not to sing the arias that her sisters practiced, she was driven to gather melodies from other sources. Mounting a chair she would give impromptu programs of them.

Plays of her own invention alternated in favor with these recitals. Often she enacted an array of characters pieced out of fragments from her busy mind. The photograph gallery next door, where she was allowed to play on hot afternoons when sitters were few, made with its painted scenes an enchanted stage for the future Isolde and Brünnhilde of two worlds.

Madame Nordica, in the opening chapter of *Hints to Singers*, speaks of still earlier and her very first essays in singing. These memories were the only ones that she retained of her birthplace, Farmington, Maine. Shortly afterward, the family removed to Boston, chiefly to secure further training for her next older sister, Wilhemina, whose voice had already received public recognition.

Those first years in Boston held singularly little for Lillian Norton. There were long walks with her father, when he explained the things about them; occasional visits to the Boston Museum; a little garden at home where flowering weeds were as dear to her as roses.

One glorious afternoon there came a break in routine; she and her sisters were taken by their father to hear the *prima donna* Parepa Rosa, and Brignoli, the tenor, in *Il Trovatore*. The group sat in the uppermost gallery, for there were so many tickets to buy. In order to

1

see, Lillian had to stand up; her eyes would just reach above the gallery railing. Peering past the chandelier from those dizzy heights, she got her first glimpse of the realm she was to enter later.

Two strange coincidences were connected with that performance. Leonora, the role sung by Parepa Rosa, was the first that Nordica studied for opera; Brignoli, whom she viewed far below, was the artist who, years afterward, appeared with her in concert on her New York debut in 1877.

Nordica's general education came largely from travel, observation, and association. Of school, she once declared to me, she was never fond. At thirteen, her days there ended. At that age, and shortly following Wilhemina's death, she entered the New England Conservatory.

Her four years of experience there, under the teaching of John O'Neill, appear to have been hard ones, stained with tears and sodden with discouragement. But they brought a vocal foundation so lasting that her whole future was securely built upon it.

One afternoon early in that period, the girl's heart glowed at a discovery; the top floor of the building which the school then occupied was separated only by a grill from Music Hall. By slight effort she slipped through and heard Rubinstein, then in his prime, play in a way never to be forgotten, as, huddled in a dark corner, she listened motionless for fear some of the beauty of it might escape her. Von Bülow and other great ones she heard, too, from the same obscure corner, always keeping the secret of her entrance lest the glorious moments be deprived her.

Life to her in those four years meant but one thing—to become a great singer. Thought of all else but study had been put aside; the joys of girlhood did not come her way; an evening party she had never known. Telling me of those years Madame Nordica inferred no recrimination, only shedding a few tears at their memory, and due to a woman's knowledge of what youth should have justly claimed.

During Lillian Norton's student days, an engagement came to her as soloist at Temple Church, bringing with it the proud independence of earning. Twelve months later, and aged sixteen, she was singing the soprano solo parts in oratorio and cantata, a new work every week, at Dr. Putnam's Church.

Of a single break in arduous routine she spoke to me more than once, for it had meant to her the awakening of patriotism. She went for a brief visit to Martha's Vineyard. An ancestor of hers, Thomas Mayhew, had owned that tract, together with Nantucket and the

Elizabeth Isles. In 1761 he was made Governor of the Province which they constituted. Earlier still, this same Thomas Mayhew had been appointed by England as first missionary to the Indians.

At the time of her girlhood visit she learned to know many of Governor Mayhew's descendents, the Allens, her mother's family, and the Nortons, her father's people. From them she heard traditions of the hardship against which her ancestors had fought in aiding to found a nation, and the service they had done in Indian wars and the War of the Revolution. She heard, too, of kindred struggles that her people had met conqueringly as pioneers in the State of Maine.

The knowledge burned into her heart. This was by sacred right *her* country too! In spite of years of residence abroad, and of splendid successes there, Madame Nordica remained through it all unalterably and inalienably an American.

Soon after the girl's return to Boston, Madame Tietjens, the dramatic *prima donna*, arrived there to sing in opera. She asked to hear any of unusual talent studying at the New England Conservatory. Lillian Norton was sent as representative. Tietjens' verdict, simply given, was, "Work ahead and you will be great."

One practical result was yielded by the visit. Among her listeners that day had been Madame Maretzek, widow of the impresario, and who, herself, had been a *prima donna*, but was then struggling on as harpist in the orchestra. She offered to coach the young singer in operatic roles at her home on Staten Island. The offer was accepted. A first flight into the world followed, Mrs. Norton, as ever after while strength lasted, accompanying her daughter, who was trained by Madame Maretzek in twelve operas of the old Italian repertory.

The next autumn Lillian Norton made her New York debut in a concert at Madison Square Garden with Gilmore's Band, then in midsuccess. The following spring she was fairly launched as soloist of the organization in a tour throughout this country, subsequently accompanying it to Europe in the same capacity.

At this point the letters of Mrs. Norton take up the story of succeeding years of study and early appearances in opera. The first letter, from Brussels, and to the family in Boston, is dated July 1, 1878. At its writing Lillian Norton's tour as soloist with Gilmore's Band neared completion. The situation is told in these paragraphs:

"We have been away from home eight weeks. Lillian has sung in sixty-five concerts, and we have travelled three thousand miles since landing in Liverpool, which, taken altogether, makes a great two months' work. . . . Lillian has sung with great success so far. I am anxious for next Thursday, July fourth, as that will close her engagement and will cap the climax. Having sung in all the great cities of England and Scotland, also in Dublin and in Holland, if she does well in Paris at the Trocadero then she will feel ready to settle down and study—and prepare to fill other engagements. She has already received letters from managers in London. Still, we cannot yet say what course we shall take until after July."

The moto of the pair seems to have been, "He who goes slowly, goes safely." All offers were held in abeyance to the Paris verdict.

"I have been looking all morning for a letter I had finished concerning Paris," writes Mrs. Norton to her daughter, Mrs. William F. Baldwin, under date of July 16, 1878. "Nowhere can I find it, greatly to my disgust, for I had taken a great deal of trouble to describe things to you in my humble way."

However, this notice from the *American Register,* Paris, was preserved: The American vocalist, Miss Lillian Norton, who accompanied them [Gilmore's Band] on their tour, has a very charming voice and, personally, is a captivating specimen of American beauty.

From the general import of this letter, decision had been reached that Lillian Norton should remain in Paris to prepare for opera, for it proceeds:

"Now, that you may know exactly what we are doing, I shall keep strictly to the subject. We have succeeded in getting the greatest teacher of dramatic action, Delsarte. It is an almost impossible thing to secure his instruction on account of scores of applications from every quarter. Lilly is also taking lessons in French, two hours every day. . . . She learns very rapidly. It remains to be seen what she can do in dramatic art. At any rate, she has the best teacher known. He says that her voice is remarkable, and that her method is perfect.

"Delsarte is a musician, and when he requested Lilly to sing an aria from *Lucia* he accompanied her. She sang with the unction which we may depend upon. Turning, he asked *what* she wished to learn. She modestly replied that she knew nothing of acting. He told her that it was in her, and, much as his time was occupied, he would *make* time to instruct her. Now, it is study in good earnest. . . .

"Tell Mr. O'Neill that Lilly is studying French and acting. Of course she must know the language to understand her teacher, and we cannot yet tell how long it will be best for her to stay here. No person has ever found one word of fault with the voice or method. But as she sees more of the world, she discovers for herself what has already been told her many times, that there is a certain scientific knowledge of motion, presence, bearing, in a word the science of grace, with which none of us is by nature overburdened."

Very early there appeared misgivings in regard to money which seemed to "melt," no matter how much care was exercised. This, dated Paris, August 25, 1878, was written to the family, and runs:

"Lilly wants very much to go to Italy, as it is the advice from all sides to get a perfect knowledge of the language, also that indefinable something which one hears and sees in all the best artists. I do not feel competent to advise, but shall let her act according to her own instincts. All I shall do is to *stand by*, which is no small part. Lilly is very good and very steady at her work. Sometimes I am afraid she will do too much.

"But money melts, at the rate of forty or fifty dollars a week. Her future is *great*, but she cannot jump into next year. She must creep and plod.

"You would be surprised to hear the progress she has made in one month in *Lucia, Traviata*, and *Faust*. But she must have time to learn all these things.

"Now, as she does not propose to marry *anyone* for helping her, the question is, can she raise three, five, seven hundred or a thousand dollars to get the requisite teaching? Belari and Randegger [as coaches], for instance, will give her lessons rather than that such a voice should stop, but Delsarte is poor and must be paid, and the French teacher is a poor woman who depends upon her pay; the ladies who keep the *pensions* have to collect their pay once a week to live.

"Hats, gloves, boots, and suitable dresses have to be replaced often, for Lilly is hard on her clothing; these are the legitimate expenses and amount to no less than thirty, forty and sometimes fifty dollars a week. As I keep account of every week's expenses, I know exactly how the money *melts*, as Lilly says."

The succeeding letter, telling of the young singer's intensive study, was written to her father, Mr. Edwin Norton, and dated Paris, September 10, 1878:

"It is no child's play to learn an opera. If you think so, listen to five or six hours of digging at Aïda every day, besides two hours French verbs. . . .

"Lilly has done an immense amount of work in the last four months, taking into account the seventy concerts. Since the twelfth of

August she has had about forty lessons with Belari [in Italian repertory]; the same number or more from Delsarte in dramatic action, besides her French lesson every day.

"I take care of everything connected with her dress and wait upon her by inches, because I know that she is doing all she can consistently. She sings most charmingly, and could, if at home, no doubt have all that she could do. But the question now is, study!!! . . .

"Lilly commences at nine o'clock every morning, a preparatory lesson in acting; at ten a pianist from Belari comes to the house to assist her in learning the notes and Italian of operas; at half past eleven she practises until twelve, then breakfasts; then French for two hours; at three music study; at four acting with Delsarte. So her whole time is occupied. She generally lies on the sofa while studying or reciting French and in that way gets rested. . . .

"The truth of the matter is, Lilly can be *great,* but she must have time to study without injury to her health, just the same as others have done. Belari, although he wants the credit of having her make her debut in Madrid, says she must not hurry too fast. She will go with me to the country for a week very soon. She has not taken a moment's rest this year. So we will leave everything behind, for a few days, and go to a country house, eat fruit, and drink milk."

The following, also to Mr. Norton, is dated Paris, October 27, 1878, and says: "We have made no material change in the plan Lilly has adopted, that is of getting the Delsarte method of dramatic action, studying French, and operas. She is still at work, early and late, on *Faust, Aïda, Lucia,* etc.

"She has done wonders in French; is able to understand all general conversation, and speaks remarkably well for only three months of study." Of her own study of the language, and to better assist her daughter, Mrs. Norton, then past fifty, makes this modest mention: "I went yesterday with Mrs. L——, of Lynn, to interpret for her in the shops. I shall not say anything of my own acquirements, but if you have any curiosity to know how much I have accomplished in three months, you can see Mrs. L—— on her return. . . .

"You cannot imagine the racket that I have to hear from morning till night. Lilly gives a lesson at nine; sings opera with a pianist from ten to eleven; gives a lesson from eleven to twelve, then we go to breakfast; then she gives a lesson from two to three; goes to a lesson with Delsarte at four, and comes home to practise one, two and three hours. Between it all I have as much as I can bear. She obliges me to

go out and get a rest from these everlasting exercises, but I do not like
to go alone. . . .

"Mr. C—— wrote advising Lilly not to work too hard, etc., etc.
Advice is good, but it is another thing to be the individual who has
to make the most of every minute and every dollar in a foreign country, in order to come within reasonable expense and make the greatest improvement in the shortest possible time. . . . With what we
have so generously received from home and what Lilly earns we
shall get along well for some time yet. I don't want Billy [Mr. William
F. Baldwin] to feel that he is throwing away his money, for we shall
do the best we can to accomplish all that is possible with as little as
possible."

This first allusion to the generous interest of Mr. Baldwin, who
married the great singer's sister Annie Norton, is followed by others
in later letters, showing his firm belief in the girl's powers, and
unselfish furtherance of her opportunities.

The next letter, to Mr. Norton, undated, but received in Boston,
December 12, 1878, was written from Milan, Italy. It contains a
prophetic estimate of the young singer's voice, given by San Giovanni,
to whom she had gone for coaching in her operatic roles; it also tells
the reason which prompted Mrs. Norton and her daughter to leave
Paris:

"San Giovanni is the head of the Conservatory in Milan, but he
gives Lilly her lessons privately in our own room every day at half-
past three. He says she has the ability to make a great dramatic singer.
He told her to-day that she must not sing any German music, because
her whole natural inclination was toward the sustained, heavy music.
Therefore, she must confine herself entirely to the Italian operatic
idea. Then she could do all that is required of a great artist. He does
not say these things for money, for he gets none! . . .

"The great necessity is time enough. It makes us uneasy when we
think how little any of our friends at home realize what it is to sit, day
in and day out, digging at opera in a foreign language. . . .

"As far as America is concerned, there is not one in five hundred
who knows whether a person sings the Italian words right or not, but
it will never do in Italy, and, sure as you live, there is nothing better
than Italian prestige.

"Lilly was told in London to be sure, with her voice, to make an
Italian reputation. But as these are *finishing* teachers, she proposed to
make a study of a few operas in Paris with a dramatic instructor. Our

plan was to study with the lamented Delsarte for six months or until January sixteenth, and then come here. But Delsarte broke down in health, and when we found his case hopeless we did not wait three days, but came here immediately.

"San Giovanni declares she has nothing to do but to commit to memory the works she has gone through, viz., *Trovatore, Norma, Lucia, Aïda* (last of all as he does not like it for a young voice), *Rigoletto, Faust, Linda, Puritani, Traviata,* and *Huguenots.*

"If you do not believe this is a work sufficient to call out all the energies of any Norton to learn or any Amanda Norton to listen to, then I do not know of what I speak, after six months of experience."

On December 12, 1878, and to Mr. Norton, his wife writes: "San Giovanni says Lilly has nothing to do but learn her operas, and that her voice, manner, figure, face and perfect simplicity insure her, with good health, of the greatest fame attached to lyric and dramatic opera. He is surprised that she sings both the *Lucia* and the *Aïda,* music so different in character. He also says that she can render the greatest operas of the age if she keeps on, but that she must have sufficient time at it, as it is as impossible to accomplish the mighty work by cramming as it would be to make a man of a boy of twelve years. Hundreds have gone through this man's hands and he knows whereof he speaks.

"His assurance to her is that next autumn she will make her debut. Sometimes, though, when we think, we feel as if we should flee. The distance between us and home! The work ahead!! The critical world!!! The expense!!!! The danger of losing health!!!!! And then the annoyance of foreign living and everything else. It would rob me of my sleep if I had not the will of a giant. But I find myself saying, 'We have gone too far to give it up.'

"Just this minute a lovely lady stepped in at our door and presented Lilly with six pairs of elegant gloves of the most delightful shades— as a birthday present. I was saying only this morning that we had shoes and stockings enough for the winter, and I guessed we could get along for gloves—and how curious that just what she wanted came right to her. O, she is a lucky girl!"

The opening words of Mrs. Norton's letter from Milan, dated December 15, 1878, and to Mrs. Baldwin, are of sound logic regarding the nourishment of singers. She writes: "I am enclosing you the menus of two dinners, so you will see that we are not starving in Italy. It would be very unwise to do differently. One never meets a teacher but who at once advises 'live well and be very careful of health,' for so many come here thinking to brave everything because they are young. . . . Lilly has commenced *Linda*. It remains for her to travel on slowly but surely till she is ready, in a year or two, as the case may be, to show what downright study can do for her development. San Giovanni's opinion is that she is young for her years, and that she will not mature or harden before twenty-four or twenty-five. She has the ability to commit to memory rapidly, but it does not do to cram the brain so as to interfere with sleep. She has a voice of the old school of Malibran, Grisi, and Tietjens. But she must not, until it is fully grown, do anything to shock the structure in which it dwells. *These* are the reasons why she is not in concert or opera, but studying judiciously and with a purpose."

Of the absolute wisdom of this course of going slowly in preparatory study, and the haste shown by young, immature singers of a later period, Madame Nordica, herself, said in the height of her career: "In the days when I began to sing, singing had not yet grown to be a business as it is now, when people are turned out in a given time as finished and equipped. I could sing the high Do in Rossini's *Inflammatus* as well then as to-day; but nobody thought anything of it. There was no rush to get my photographs for the papers, and columns were not written about me. I had to grow up in music gradually and with patient toil. And that is the only way. There should be small, cautious, conscientious beginnings; the doing of all things to the limit of one's ability, and a gradual growth. *Then* the career will take care of itself."

Mrs. Norton, in this same letter dwelling mainly upon the singing art, writes a brief paragraph holding flash of pathos: "I had the black silk cloak turned so that it looks as good as new. We are having nothing new this winter, as we are very closely at home, only going to the lessons every day."

Toward the close another item is discussed, the stage name of the young singer, who, up to then, had sung as Lillian Norton. It was San Giovanni who settled this, a matter the importance of which the mother seemed scarcely to have realized, for she writes: "Oh! I almost forgot to tell you that San Giovanni has been studying names, and says that the name of Norton signifies North, which in old languages was Nord or Nort; in the Italian Norte. Therefore the name, to be euphonious to the Italians, must be Norteca or Nordiga or Nordica. One of these, he asserts, should be her stage name; making it more easy to the ear of foreigners, who always pronounce it so one would

hardly know it, on account of the long o in both syllables. Hereafter
we shall decide such trivial questions which require no study."

In writing from Milan, December 26, 1878, and to her husband,
Mrs. Norton opens with the pathetic sentence: "The Christmas of
another year is past, and it was a day of all others the most fraught
with memories." But these memories she does not give herself the luxury to dwell upon, turning quickly to her self-imposed mission. This
time she defends a stage to which their daughter had dedicated her
life, and which the father still, perhaps, regarded with Puritan misgivings: "Mr. R—— sent Lilly his disquisition on opera singers. After
thoroughly reading it twice I concluded he must have seen and known
a great deal more of the stage than we ever *have* or ever *shall*. Lilly
has sung in many of the largest theatres and halls in America, Great
Britain, Holland, Belgium, and finally in the French metropolis at the
Trocadero, and much of that time travelled with sixty-five gentlemen
of all nationalities, that is, German, Italian, French, Irish, and
American. And not one word or look was ever heard or seen in the
least possible manner approaching disrespect. Not a man of Gilmore's
Band would do more than raise his hat in complete deference to us as
we met them in hotels, theatres or the street. As for Mr. Gilmore, he
has the bearing and the soul of a Christian gentleman.

"*No matter what the calling,* you can find plenty of disaster, ruin,
and corruption. Every woman can stand on her own self-made reputation, whether in church, state, or on the stage."

In another Milan letter, and dated January 16, 1879, she spurs his
courage with her own: "Pupils do not come here and make a career in
six weeks or six months. If anyone thinks so, put the opera of *Aïda* or
Norma before them, and let them report when they have it ready for
an audience. There is a great deal of talk, and there are a great many
voices, but only one out of a thousand is heard of outside their own
town or city. Fifteen thousand pupils have been graduated from the
New England Conservatory, and *not one* has the reputation already
made by Lilly in America, Great Britain, and France, and finally will
have made in Italy. Mark my word. Cheer her with every good word
and deed, as you always have done, and joy will fill your cup of
patience."

Items of interest are mentioned by Mrs. Norton in her next letter to
her husband, dated January 23, 1879. One is that their daughter, who
has had forty lessons with San Giovanni, is studying *Norma,* and that
in his opinion she will make a *Norma* such as there are very few to-day.

With her inborn caution, however, the mother adds, "It must take great experience to give this opera acceptably. It may never be done by Lilly, but we shall wait and see.

"San Giovanni states that Lilly has the voice and the disposition (meaning the intelligence), which are worth more than all the knowledge of music reading in the world. He declares that the pupils who come to him ready to read everything at first sight, nine times out of ten run all to the science, but miss the grand secret—feeling. His words are, 'Give me pupils of intelligence, and they will move the hearts of their listeners, while the musician will develop more probably into a good teacher or composer.' "

From Milan, on January 26, 1879, the following was written to her daughter, Mrs. Baldwin: "Lilly still likes her *maestro* very much and is going ahead in her studies as fast as is allowable. Her voice is called very heavy and dramatic, but she is cautioned not to sing too much. You will see by the papers that Miss Marco [Smith] is told by her physician not to sing for one year to come. She studied with San Giovanni and he says was a very nice singer, but took an engagement at St. Petersburg in *Lohengrin*, being very ambitious to make a career suddenly, and spoiled her voice.

"Another singer, a Hungarian, was preparing for opera with him since we came here, and was ready, but was taken ill. Still she persisted in singing, when her teacher told her that if she would wait one week she could go through with the engagement all right. But she was headstrong, and commenced the opera season in an Italian city of some note. She broke down completely, although she had a dramatic soprano voice, and the manager was obliged to close the opera house as he could not find another Norma.

"They want to present *Il Trovatore* at La Scala and have tried twenty-seven voices, but no one has been engaged yet. I am telling you these things to show how scarce dramatic singers are, and that to become first class ones they have to make haste slowly or the voice will exhaust the body. . . . We have settled with the landlord to-day for all we owe him up to this time, and I have counted over what still remains. We shall have enough for the next month. The wood bill was nine dollars, the washing eight, so with the board we paid him one hundred and seventeen dollars. . . . Since writing last Lilly has commenced the study of *Huguenots* and is mastering it. . . . Do you realize that it is nearly a year since we left you? We were just saying that it made our heads swim to think that we were so long and so far from home. It is a great thing for two women to come alone to the old world and buffet its customs, its climates, and its foods. However, we have been good for it, so far, and with continued health shall be.

"Be of good courage at home, each side of the ocean has its obstacles to surmount, and if you will pull with a long and a strong pull, we shall do the same, and all will be well. We do the best we know how, sure that in the end (which by the way never comes), the summit we are climbing now will, when reached, reveal new ones perhaps higher."

This letter, sent by Mrs. Norton from Milan to her husband, under date of February 7, 1879, carried news justifying optimism: "San Giovanni has proposed Lilly, after two months' study with him, to a manager in Milan, and says he would not have done it if he were not confident of her ability. . . .

"Already she has two offers to sing in two cities in Italy. If you could see the facts as we do, you would very quickly realize that she is one in a thousand. These engagements are not remunerative but *tests* and give prestige. Carl Rosa, Strackosch, Mapleson, and many others come here every year to search for material. Unless the pupils have been tested, how can a teacher offer them to impresarios?

"As sure as we are granted health, everything will come out all right. It is a mighty undertaking, *full as much* as I ever imagined; but we are good for it. I am just the woman to go through thick and thin to fulfill a mission. And Lilly is just the girl to accomplish what she has started for."

The succeeding, addressed to Mrs. Baldwin by her mother and dated February 11, 1879, tells of closing the Milan contract: "Lilly has signed to sing in opera, through the recommendation of San Giovanni. . . . Of course, the first requisite to success is a *voice,* but the *next* is to fall into the right hands.

"The appearances will be what is here called a *prova.* In reality a test to settle exactly the ability of the person whom impresarios may hereafter recommend at a stipulated price to managers, coming for material to this great musical business center. . . .

"Almost all singers have to pay for a debut; in Lilly's case all the wardrobe is found, except that she prefers to use her own gloves and boots.

"She received a very pleasant letter to-day from Mr. C—— in which he wishes that she would go home and take the position of soprano in Dr. Webb's church, and sing in concert and oratorio. He says they would give her a good salary. He also said that she could have sung in the *Messiah* better than the one who did etc., etc. He is not sanguine of her singing in opera, although he says he has no doubt of her success. But she will make the attempt on the eighth of March! And if her forte is *not* opera, she feels sure of oratorio, etc. We shall wait and work and hope for the best."

In this, from Milan, February 20, 1879, and to her daughter, Mrs. George A. Walker, mention is made of a second engagement: "The first, in Milan, March eighth, is in the opera of *Don Giovanni* as Donna Elvira. I do not know any of the other artists except Faggotti, the baritone, although I hear that they are good. The Donna Anna is a Hungarian; the Zerlina a Pole, and Lilly, the debutante, the only American. So you see the plot begins to thicken when a young lady with three months of study in Milan can appear in one of the finest theatres [Manzoni] in that city as *prima donna*.

"Her second engagement is at Brescia, a very nice musical city on the Gulf of Venice. She has given the refusal of her services as Violetta in *Traviata,* and if the management secure such other talent as they wish, the opera will be in April."

Dated February 24, 1879, there is this, also to Mrs. Walker: "Lilly has engagements to sing a month in Milan, off and on, in two other operas, also in Brescia in April; it will be doubtful about our going to Naples. She wishes to give the summer to a perfect mastery of the language. Still, we cannot tell what may be, as Brignoli has written her not to make any long engagements as he will procure her advantageous opportunities. Her stage name, Giglio Nordica, is at San Giovanni's direction, and I hope all will be pleased at home. . . .

"Lilly will commence rehearsals at the theatre on the twenty-sixth. San Giovanni says he has no fears for her, but that the first rehearsal with orchestra will be her greatest trial. She has learned the whole opera of *Don Giovanni* in two weeks."

Rehearsals for Nordica's first appearance at the Manzoni Theatre are mentioned in a letter to Mrs. Baldwin, dated March first: "We were at rehearsal this noon, and the director said that Lilly knew her part perfectly and could be free from rehearsal this evening. . . . San Giovanni is sanguine of her success. Although her part is not the first, he says it is just the thing to begin with, without any pretensions and without trumpeting. It will very soon be acknowledged who has the voice. She is given credit for what they call a 'delicious' pronunciation.

"Lilly does not have time for anything but to eat—sleep—

rehearse—and give two lessons every day and take one of the *maestro*. I, in the meantime, keep myself ready for all emergencies, which are not few. I am not at all troubled about her not singing all right, but the theatre is so damp, the hours so late, that I am always on the watch to see that she does not take cold, or get hungry or over-worked."

On March 9, 1879, Mrs. Norton wrote a general family letter, telling of the opera's postponement: "Lilly was to have appeared last night in *Don Giovanni,* but on account of the illness of Zerlina, it has been put off two days. So she will make her debut to-morrow night, March tenth. The Italians give plenty of rehearsals; for instance, in this case they had no less than twenty, fifteen with piano, five with orchestra.

"It is hard work for every one. Not one of the artists allows herself or himself to be absent from two rehearsals daily. They show the nicest consideration for Lilly, giving every hint and suggestion that they could give to one of their own nationality. She says, however, that she never could have done it, but for her study with Delsarte. . . . The way she sings *Ah perfido!* fills every nook of the theatre. . . . Now, while Lilly is to sing from two to five times a week, she is studying *Traviata* every day with San Giovanni; has a pianist three times a week to play for her, also a lady teacher to give her the *scena.* . . . There are never any fires in the theatres in Italy, which at this season are very damp and chilly. So I take a hot brick every night, and when Lilly is not occupied, I have it ready for her feet."

Of the debut, Mrs. Norton wrote to her husband on the day suc-ceeding it, March 11, 1879: "Lilly sand last night with fine success. There were three *prima donna* sopranos, and both the others were hissed. . . . Lilly made a correct rendering of the music in time, tune, and pronunciation. San Giovanni says to-day, as do many others, that she may well be gratified with her debut in Milan. . . . It was terrible to hear the others hissed and howled, and it required moral courage for Lilly to appear after the leading *prima donna* had been screamed at, 'Enough! Enough!' but Lilly came out of the ordeal conqueror. . . . The tenth of April we shall go to Brescia to commence rehearsals for *Traviata.*"

The hissing and howling mentioned had brought, and quickly, sad results. Of these, Mrs. Norton wrote to Mrs. Baldwin on March 16, 1879: "The impresarios and managers held a meeting, and after look-ing the situation over, reached the following decision, viz., that

Nandori, Faggotti, and Corsi, the three principal actors and artists in the affair, be utterly discarded and that Nordica, Lombardelli (basso), Tessada (basso comico), and the tenor, Niviani, be retained. But it is impossible at a minute's notice to procure a Don Giovanni, a Donna Anna, and a Zerlina. So the opera is laid up for the present. But remember, it is through no fault of Lilly. . . . If she had failed, she could not have kept the engagement at Brescia, for it is her reputation from Milan that secures her there. All the papers give Lilly credit for voice, time, tune, and sympathy. . . . In the ensembles she had to wade as best she could. But when she sang alone, she was applauded."

Of the reasons for Nordica's success, Mrs. Norton said to her husband under date of March 20, 1879: "There is but one school of singing in the world, and that is the Italian. No matter what language you wish to sing in, what style of music you wish to study, the voice must be trained and used in the Italian method if one hopes to deserve the name of singer. Such is Mr. O'Neill's method, and it was his training that gave Lilly an early start here in the midst of all that is musical. All the papers speak of her unexceptionable method."

Without further regret or recrimination, the incident seems quite to have been lost sight of in hopes ahead. A letter by Mrs. Norton to Mrs. Baldwin, from Brescia, April 24, 1879, says: "The whole city is agog to hear the American *prima donna,* as it is noised about by the papers and the orchestra that she has *una bella voce.* I have no fears of the result. Still, I am quite anxious for the first representation to be over, and to hear the verdict of the people. I can only judge that all is well by the rounds of applause from the orchestra during rehearsals. . . . Now, as to ourselves, we would gladly go home this summer, but it would cost too much. Besides, Lilly would have to come back for her fall engagements, which she considers of the utmost importance. This is the country for the young artist to get experience in opera. There are so many opera houses here, and a person with talent can be put right ahead.

"If a girl studies in Italy three or six years and does not amount to much, you may be sure that something is the matter, for the demand for good singers here is as great as in America, and the facilities for putting them on the stage far greater. The people, if they have not another shirt to their backs, go to the opera. Therefore, opera is sustained at reasonable prices. Italy is the country for art, but for money, don't mention it!!!"

A letter dated Brescia, April 27, 1879, and headed by Mrs. Norton,

"My dear family in America," describes the real debut of Lillian Nordica: "Last night was the first appearance of your absent Lilly in *Traviata* and I have only to repeat what the crowded theatre demonstrated, people standing in mass giving rounds of applause and *bravas* that would have done your heart good.

"I am repaid for a year's anxiety when I see the musical public of the second city in Lombardy calling imperatively, *'bis! bis!! bis!!!'* till she was nine times before the curtain with a smile and gracious acknowledgment for all, from the proscenium boxes to the gallery.

"Only think of men and women sobbing as though they were actually witnessing the death of a beautiful girl, who struggles to live, yet must die. The most convincing point of all was, that tears ran down her cheeks as she bade adieu to all the joys of life. After this, when she returned before the curtain, loaded with flowers of exquisite colors, it seemed as though the public would go mad.

"The owner of the opera house and impresario came immediately to her dressing-room, and gave every possible graceful acknowledgment of her artistic rendering of their beloved *Traviata*. This morning at ten o'clock a string band came under her windows at the hotel and commenced playing the overture to *Traviata*. After finishing it, there were calls for *Nordica! Bellissima Violetta!* When she went to the window a hundred persons were waiting, and they just rent the air with *La Americana Nordica! La gentilissima Violetta!* San Giovanni and many others from Milan have come to hear to-night's performance. I know you must think me egotistical, but I am so far from home, and on such a responsible errand, that it would not be strange if I became quite absorbed in the results of the year's work.

"I have no leisure, any more than if I were employed in a manufacturing house. It is one continuous routine of clearing up the room, getting ready to go to rehearsal (for nothing is done in this country, as a rule, without thorough preparation); then, mending, cutting things over, turning them upside down and inside out; making beef tea, going to walk to get the fresh air indispensable to the singer, and, when Lilly is asleep, as she is now, sitting still as a mouse, and all in a climate that is inclined to debilitate. I tell you it is work. Then comes the night of the opera, dresses to be arranged to take to the theatre, and changed four times for the several acts."

There follows a description of the costumes, some of which were made by Mrs. Norton herself, and of jewels loaned by Mrs. Marcia Roosevelt-Scovel, a wealthy New Yorker, whose husband had also made his debut as Alfredo in the season's opening performance of *Traviata* at the Teatro Guillaume, Brescia.

At the letter's close there is this message from the young debutante to her Boston teacher: "Lilly says to write to Mr. O'Neill that she has never swerved from his method and teaching, and she also wishes, no matter what may go into the papers, that he may be given his credit."

The next letter is to Mr. Norton, and dated May 2, 1879: "What better news could I write than that we are in good health, and that Lilly has already appeared four times in *Traviata,* to packed houses. The impresario is wild with delight to think that his venture has proved so successful.

"She sang on the twenty-sixth and twenty-seventh of April, also on the twenty-ninth, and the first day of May. She will sing again on the fourth, which will be the anniversary of our sailing from New York one year ago. The season will close on the fourteenth; her benefit will be on the tenth.

"It is impossible for me to give you an adequate idea of the perfect delight with which Lilly is greeted by a crowded house, the people in the audience standing on their feet and leaning out of the boxes shouting, *Brava! Bravissima!*"

The following naïve, girlish letter by Lillian Nordica to her father shows her equilibrium under sudden elevation. It is dated Brescia, May 3, 1879: "Dear Father: Mother has written, I suppose at some length, on my great success in opera. Well, she cannot say too much. I have had a grand success and no mistake. Such yelling and shouting you never heard. The theatre is packed. I put right into the acting, and you would not know me. It makes me laugh to see men and women cry and wipe their noses in the last act. Just wait, if nothing happens we will show old —— something.

"I am going to sing *Faust* in September at Monza, which I hope will go well. Do send the papers oftener. Sometimes it does seem as if I should die off with nothing to read in English. I am obliged to read French and Italian.

"I shall hurry home as soon as possible. It is rather lonesome sometimes, I assure you. Of course Annie [her sister, Mrs. Baldwin] will call him Roberto: I think Southwick is just elegant. Next Saturday night is my benefit. I shall sing the Mad Scene from *Lucia* extra. My dresses are all very nice, and I cut a swell. Well, good-night. It was one o'clock last night when I got to bed. Lillie."

An incident of the love of music inspiring the young *prima donna*'s listeners is told in a letter enclosing hers to Mr. Norton: "Two women walked fourteen miles to hear *Traviata*, and in that way saved their little stock of *lire* to pay for entrance tickets. After the performance, they begged of the janitor to let them sleep in the opera house, as they had not a cent to pay for lodgings. He very kindly gave them a bed in his small apartment.

"The next morning they started back on their fourteen-mile tramp, fully satisfied, they said, for all their trouble, as they had never before heard such a *Violetta*. If Lilly had known of this in season, she would have given them a few *lire*."

An item, practical in import, follows: "Another thing I wish to say is that we have $150.00 by us, and we feel that we are being just as prudent as possible. I shall owe fifty dollars the 7th of May, and after paying it shall be square with all debts, and have one hundred dollars left. Don't you think that is coming out at the end of the year pretty well?"

Through hot summer days, mother and daughter remained at their post in Milan; the young *prima donna* toiling ahead with a single aim inspiring her. During that period, Mrs. Norton's letters, briefly quoted, throw sidelights on her daughter's progress and on the Italian operatic situation.

The inside history of Nordica's debut at Brescia, and the fact that she paid for it through her independent effort, is told to Mr. Norton in these words: "At Brescia they also wanted a tenor, and to put two debutantes on the stage at the risk of their making a successful season, they required one thousand *lire*, to pay the municipality, the owner of the theatre, etc., as the impresario was not worth a cent, but said to be an honest man.

"Well, Mr. Scovel [an American tenor], was very ambitious to make a musical career, and, on San Giovanni's advice, advanced the money. But Lilly did not wish to put herself under any obligation to him, so she arranged with the impresario that if she proved a success she was to have a benefit, which means in this country to receive half the profits after all expenses are paid. She did prove a success, had the benefit, and turned the money over to Mr. Scovel."

Madame Nordica, herself, in *Hints to Singers,* speaks of this curious method prevailing in Italy and of the logic of it in existing circumstances, advising young aspirants to accept the situation as did she.

Under date of July fourth in the same summer, Mrs. Norton gives a glimpse of the intrigue of Italian music publishers. Her words stating the situation are: "Two publishing houses, Ricordi and Lucca, own all the operas for Italy, and are always in a fight. Not an opera can be given unless from five thousand to eight or eleven thousand *lire* are paid to the house that owns the work.

"First, Lucca owns in Italy the rights to *Faust*, and also wants a new opera to be given at Monza in the same season. But the management is afraid of the new opera and does not wish to produce it. So Lucca says, 'Unless you give it, you shall not have *Faust*.' Whereupon the manager says, 'I will give *Traviata* and some other opera from Ricordi.' Lucca flares up, and answers, 'I live in Monza and have a great many influential relatives there, and *I* will do all I can to hurt your artists in *Traviata*.'

"We do not say one word, but entrust the whole matter to San Giovanni, who knows all the ins and outs, and will look after the good of his own pupils every time."

From this, and from many another instance of which she speaks, Mrs. Norton proved diplomatic judgment equal to any situation, although reared on a farm and plunged into the foreign vortex with no experience in any city save Boston, with its American methods, so entirely different. "It is uphill business," she states, "so is everything that succeeds. Annie Cary stayed here till she had not a cent left, because she said she knew she needed the style of Italy or rather of Italian singing."

The sequel of the pretty quarrel between publisher and impresario is told a few days later to her daughter Mrs. Baldwin: "Caseau, the impresario, would not risk the new opera with a company proposed by Lucca, and has taken another theatre in the principal city of Piedmont. Will give you the name in my next, as I do not know how to spell it. He has engaged Lilly to sing Alice in *Roberto Il Diavolo*. Of course, she will be a debutante in the opera; still they pay her something, and while a dozen girls would pay for the chance, she gets it without asking. These are straws, but they indicate the direction of the wind.

"The country, and especially Milan, is swarming with singers, some with money and no voice. They *all* get a chance to sing once, because the poor managers of theatres are ready to grab every cent they can get, and risk results with the public, which will not be cheated but once by the same voice. However, the good voice, without money, is sure to win; only give her or him time.

"Christine Nilsson had $50,000 spent on her musical education and her debuts, therefore she bounded to the front. If Lilly had only $10,000 she could sing in Rome, Naples, Florence, Venice, Genoa and finally at La Scala as fast as she could go from one engagement to another, for they (the impresarios) are so poor that they are continually looking for those who can pay for appearances. This may seem strange to you, but it is the sober truth. Lilly will have to become known solely through her merit—it is a slower process, but *sure in the end*.

"We heard the celebrated Lamperti give two lessons, and afterward he asked Lilly to sing the aria from *Lucia*. Listening attentively throughout, at its close he came forward (the tottering old man), gave her his hand in congratulation, and most kindly said in unmistakable enthusiasm, 'You are bound to make a grand artist; your voice, intonation, and trills are delicious.' The wife of Lamperti spoke up and said, 'You will be the second Tietjens.' "

It was from Milan on August 4, 1879, that Mrs. Norton in writing to her husband of their daughter's growing opportunities, announced, "Lilly has signed an engagement at Novara for December. The impresario is to pay her 550 *lire,* a very small sum, but it is not like paying it out ourselves. She may also go to Genoa in October, but not without pay, enough to cover current expenses. You may rest assured that she is all right, and knows just what she is about.

"The agent of Carl Rosa was here to see if he could possibly engage her for the coming autumn and winter, but she does not want to sing in opera in English. This morning we had a letter, saying, 'Come to London, Mapleson will pay the expenses of two at a hotel, and give Miss Lillian Norton an engagement.' Lilly will also refuse this prospect. She is *determined* to finish what she has begun so successfully, viz., to master the language, and make her repertory large and perfect."

Genoa was the next objective point in Lillian Nordica's Italian engagements and where she appeared in November, 1879, at the Politeama Genovese. Apparently several of Mrs. Norton's letters relating to this period have been lost. However, in one sent to Mrs. Baldwin, and dated Genoa, November 19, 1879, there is sufficient information to give a good idea of the season's outcome: "Long before this you have heard of the success of La Nordica. She has sung eight nights, and notwithstanding other operas have been given on the nights between her appearances, and with the well-known artist Urban, Lilly has sung to the largest houses of the season. *Faust* has, they say, been given fifty times in Genoa and by the best artists, even Patti. Yet it seems that this unknown Margherita has managed to gain the sympathy and respect of the great audience. I expect she will storm the castle when she sings *Traviata*, for it is a much more brilliant opera and suits young people better than does *Faust*. But it takes a voice well up in the *mezzo* to do it. Without the middle voice it is impossible to rank in the old school. . . .

"The critics say Lilly is an ideal Margherita, and that Goethe could have had none better in his imagination. Also, they say that she sings with excellent schooling, and has the seeds (as they express it), of a perfect artist.

"If you could realize all the points in the case as I do: the immense theatre; the competition; her youth; her short time in a foreign country; and that this is only her second theatre in an important city; you would wonder, as I do, that she has given eight representations without *one* dissenting voice. Not only that, but she has had genuine and enthusiastic applause, and been recalled many times to the proscenium.

"Gialdino Gialdini, the leader of orchestra, and noted in Italy, says that he has never heard any person of English blood sing with such soul and expression."

Those days, however, were not all glory. Only brief inkling was allowed, though, of the reverse side of the picture, Mrs. Norton being too brave to succumb. "I know," she writes to Mrs. Baldwin, "that I shall grow very old in the cause, but I don't care. I wish very much to accomplish what we started out to do, although we little knew the whole truth of it. Many times Lilly says, 'Mother, we can never tell them exactly how it is.'

"Sometimes, for a moment, we are tempted to give up the whole thing! Then again, as one must do in everything else, we take courage and go on day by day, meeting the various contingencies as they arise. And you may be sure that they are not few."

From Novara, Italy, which held the next engagement, Mrs. Norton wrote of the final days at Genoa, under date of December 15, 1879: "Lilly's benefit night at the Politeama was wonderful. She sang four acts of *Faust*, and the first act from *Traviata*, receiving an ovation of applause. There were flowers in masses; a pocket-book with one hundred *lire*, from the officers of the U.S.S. Quinnebaugh; a gold chain for her neck, and a brooch in the form of an arrow set with diamonds and pearls. . . . Lilly has gained in flesh in Genoa. I think it agrees with her to sing in opera, when she is called to the proscenium four times after singing an aria, as she was there. . . .

"She has had a telegram from Mr. de Reszke, a great basso, asking when she would be at liberty as he had a fine opportunity to offer her. He heard Lilly at Genoa, and says she is going to be a great singer. . . .

"Lilly has passed the *prova* here [Novara], before the directors and proprietor of the theatre, and was accepted on the first rehearsal. They paid her the first quarter according to contract.

"By the way, before she left the theatre on the night of her benefit at Genoa, they paid Lilly 500 *lire*. We have been told again and again that Italian impresarios never paid what they agreed to, but, so far, we have found them perfectly honorable."

Three caricatures are enclosed in a letter sent on the same day to Mrs. Baldwin; in the first of these Mrs. Norton depicts herself as a storm-worn bird; the other two, spirited in drawing, are by Nordica. The one shows her, after long years and grown to immense proportions, at last singing *Norma;* the other, muffled to the ears and wearing great galoshes, portrays her going to rehearsal in Novara's frigid cold.

The little note written by her on the back of the gay *Norma* caricature is one hinting at home longing: "This is the size I shall be by the time I sing *Norma.* I had some pictures taken in Genoa, and shall send them as soon as possible.

"By the time you receive this, Hattie will be married. I suppose you have done more shopping, selecting and running about, than could get fourteen outfits. Tell me all about what she had and everything. You don't know how lonesome it is, and cold. Oh no! Not at all—four degrees below zero in the room where I rehearse. To-night we rehearse in the theatre with our books, so I must study a little. Lillie."

Mrs. Norton's letter conveys still more clearly that same home longing, one that is breathed so often between her lines: "As it approaches Christmas, notwithstanding we are so much occupied, we think and talk of you all at home, and wish and wish that we could see you or send something to show our love. But 'it is as it is,' and we shall endeavor to abide results.

"We are entirely alone in Novara, except the casual acquaintance that we have with the various members of the company. The half can never be told of our surroundings. Straw carpet on a stone floor; thermometer seven degrees below; a fireplace no bigger than a good sized keeler to wash dishes in. It is three in the afternoon, and we have just got in from rehearsal. We have to go twice a day, blow high or blow low."

The Novara season, in which Nordica sang the Violetta in *Traviata* and Alice in *Roberto Il Diavolo*, was summed up toward the close of it by Mrs. Norton in a letter dated February 5, 1880, indited to Mrs. Baldwin, "and all": "The thirty representations of opera promised for the season will finish next Monday the tenth, so we shall go to Milan on the eleventh and see what is to be done next.

"Lilly has had great success in every way; the papers say she gives an individuality entirely her own to her roles, which pleases very much, for notwithstanding the great tendency of the Italians toward tradition, when a person is independent enough to introduce original ideas and stick to them, they will succumb. . . . She will sing three times more, probably her benefit will be the last night of the season. . . . She has earned her fee, one hundred and ten dollars. It is considered a good deal of money here! There are many who would sing for nothing, and pay, too, for the chance.

"An English woman offered the direction 2,000 *lire,* if they would let her sing *Traviata.* San Giovanni said in answer, 'We will accept it on this condition, that Nordica shall receive 1,000 *lire* and sing the first three nights.' But the English woman didn't see it in that light; she would give the money, but would not sing *after* 'the Nordica.' "

From Milan, under date of February 23, 1880, Mrs. Norton told Mrs. Baldwin of prospects in store: "The contract, which Lilly is about to make, will give her the opportunity to sing in all the great cities of the world; for instance, Naples, Rome, Turin, Florence, Venice, St. Petersburg, and also in America. . . . You can have no idea what a struggle it is to get a foothold where there is so much pulling and hauling, especially without money. But I think our feet are firmly planted on the first round of the ladder of success."

The entrance of Lillian Nordica into the great world of music and on the stage of the Imperial Italian Opera, St. Petersburg, took place the autumn following this brave assurance. On September 11, 1880, her mother wrote: "Well, Lilly has passed the first rehearsal as Filina in *Mignon,* and all doubts, if I had any, are gone. She sang with the celebrated La Sala, so much talked of, and her voice suffers no detraction.

"Now, Lilly has her first opportunity to sing with first-class artists, La Sala, Chiatti, Scalchi, Bianca, and the celebrated baritone Cotogni.

. . . I suppose I shall have the appearance of trying to convince you that Lilly is doing wonderful work! And so she is!! . . ."

The following lines from St. Petersburg were written by Mrs. Norton to her husband on October 1, 1880: "Lilly is at the piano studying the part of the Queen in *Huguenots,* to be ready for her second appearance. So it seems there is no doubt of her success in *Mignon.* . . . We were awfully homesick to-night, but the hand is put to the plow, and there is no turning back. . . . We do not have to step outside of the house this winter, except to go from the door to the carriage, and that under cover, both at the house and at the theatre. We are far better situated than in Italy last winter."

The following day she wrote: "Lilly has had a call to sing *Mignon* a third time, and you had better believe she did it without fear, and with confidence in her ability. She was repeatedly recalled. Russian audiences have a manner peculiar to themselves of calling by name the artist whom they want, and it did my old ears good to hear 'La Nordica! La Nordica!! La Nordica!!!'

"If her health is good (as it is now), and the climate is not too rigorous, she will make a great hit here, notwithstanding the celebrated artists, notwithstanding the great theatre, and the great public."

Writing to Mrs. Baldwin, October 4, 1880, Mrs. Norton says: "It was my dream from the beginning that Lillian sing here. But I never dared to tell it, after I realized the battle that there was to fight. . . . But, no thanks to anything, save the everlasting perseverance, will, and pluck of Lilly and Marmie. We have seen ourselves without a cent, but kept right on. We have never suffered for food, nor from frozen feet, and we have worked like tigers."

From the opera house, Mrs. Norton wrote to Mrs. Baldwin: "Lilly is rehearsing at this moment with the celebrated Masini in the *Huguenots,* and their voices are like silver. If she has made a success such as all say she has in *Mignon,* there is not one doubt of her future in this country, and especially when she attacks dramatic operas."

Nor were her triumphs at the opera the sole phase of happiness rewarding Lillian Nordica's strenuous efforts. In another letter her devoted mother pictures the social life of a St. Petersburg now vanished, a society that evidenced such strong appreciation of art and artists: "Refinement is always a passport to Russian society, and art a double passport. . . . We had a very pleasant visit to-day from the wife of General Tolstoi, one of the great men of Russia. She was a Princess, but lost her title by marrying out of her rank, he being a Count. He is most charming. She invited us to dine with them next Sunday, as we had no other day at liberty. Their palace is a home of exquisite luxury. She is an artist, and plays the music of Chopin as well as Essipoff."

There is also mention of the family of Madame de Richter, lady in waiting to the Czarina, "who have shown us the utmost respect and consideration, and will be among the first to make us welcome if we come back. We learned to know them through Tosti (the composer), and who told them among other charming things that Lilly was by nature a great artist.

"To-morrow night is the opera; the next a dinner at Goldenburg's, a house famous for its dinners; next day the opera; the following one at the de Richters'; Saturday we dine with them; Sunday at the Tolstois'; Monday at Colonel Gamoff's; Tuesday the opera, Wednesday the de Claus's, and so on ahead for two weeks to come.

"The educated society here is made up of most delightful families, living in luxury, and ready to render every possible delicate attention to us; such as sending their equipages, inviting us to dine, and coming to sit an hour with us in our far less luxurious rooms."

Lillian Nordica was re-engaged at the Imperial Italian Opera, St. Petersburg, having achieved in her first season there a brilliant recognition. At its close, she left the Russian capital for Paris, where she made her debut at the Grand Opéra.

"Now Billy, Annie, and Edwin," [Mr. and Mrs. Baldwin and the singer's father], writes the mother of Lillian Nordica: "I see the first rays of daylight in rosy tints just peeping above the eastern horizon. Look this way, and keep your patience. . . . The first half of the battle is fought, *and victory is ours.*"

1. Amanda Allen Norton,
Lillian Nordica's mother (date unknown)

2. Lillian Nordica as Violetta in Giacomo Puccini's
La Traviata, at the Politeama, Genoa, 1879.

3. Lillian Nordica during her first engagement
at the Imperial Opera, St. Petersburg, 1880.

4. Lillian Nordica as Sulamith in Charles Gounod's
La Reine de Saba, at the time of her London debut, 1887.

5. Lillian Nordica as Isolde
in Richard Wagner's *Tristan und Isolde*, 1895.

6. Lillian Nordica as Brünnhilde
in Richard Wagner's *Die Walküre*, 1898.

7. Lillian Nordica at the height of her career,
probably before 1900.

8. The last photograph of Lillian Nordica,
taken before she left home on her ill-fated world tour, 1913.

HINTS TO SINGERS
by Lillian Nordica

CHAPTER I

Choice of Singing as a Profession

GREAT singers are, as far as personal experience has shown me, those who have sung always. Turn back to the beginning of the career of any successful singer, Patti, Melba, Calvé, Lehmann, any one of them, indeed, that may be named, and you will find that they have sung from childhood.

The fitness for a career as a singer will not leave much room for doubt in early years, for, even before the gift of speech, the voice and inborn love of music will not infrequently be shown. Then, as time goes on, the child advances gradually, growing up in music as in stature, and in such gradual growth alone is confidence to be placed, as far as the making of a future is concerned.

Masini, the tenor, was a shoemaker, and through his beautiful voice sprang into fame in a day, but that voice had been always there, he had sung always, it was not with him a matter of beginning yesterday.

It is no more possible to awaken suddenly to find that one can sing than it would be to awaken to find that one had learned overnight to read and write. One cannot wait until one is twenty or twenty-five and start out with the sudden discovery that one has a voice.

To ask any singer just when their musical ideas began would be a question probably impossible to answer. My mother has told me that, with my head on her breast, I followed her in the singing of a scale before I could speak. There came a day when, perched on a square piano, I sang "Little Drops of Water" at a Sunday School entertainment, and promptly burst into tears instead of an encore, when the audience applauded. Memories come back to me of sitting, with other children of my mother's Sunday School class, in a row in the garden

27

on summer afternoons, with the piano drawn near the window, while she taught us. There came another day when music was introduced into the public schools of Boston, and Mr. Mason said, "Can any little girl tell me what this means?" pointing to a chart with the Do, Re, standing out in bold relief, Greek to the rest, upon it, and I was able to pipe up my proof.

Again, there came a later time when my ambitions grew and my energy as well, and my sisters were driven to pay me not to sing on appropriate and inappropriate occasions the opera or oratorio numbers they had newly learned.

True Success as a Singer is impossible to those with whom the question is "How long will it take me to get on the stage, and how much shall I make when I get there?" The mercenary feeling cannot enter into it; one must study because one loves one's art, and once having begun one must stick to it. Love of art is the secret of true study. That art is not to be looked upon as a vehicle for making money, but as a something to be done beautifully, and to be done well for its own sake alone. As to the age to begin: Every little girl who at six can sing correctly and shows a love of music should be given lessons on the piano, and, a most important factor of musical education, reading at sight, just as the a, b, c's are taught. With a good voice and ear to receive such training, it will prove a great comfort in later life, whether the course of professional or amateur may be pursued.

The First Opportunity to Prove Natural Ability in the long, slow evolution that goes to make the career of a singer, may come with the school concert, or some similar undertaking. A child whose voice has made itself distinguished among the rest will, perhaps, be chosen to sing a few bars or a little part. With this episode there is likely to be established a firmer desire to learn more. The child grows gradually into things day by day, working them out in a way impossible when once the teens are past. There may, indeed, be an extraordinary gift that renders possible a career beginning later in life than the period named, but such instance has not come under my personal observation.

For a Girl it is quite early enough to enter upon vocal training seriously when the health is established. After a period of serious study there comes as a probable result a position in a church choir, when self-consequence receives a salutary blow with the discovery of superior ability in another who has enjoyed a longer training.

With the Boy, the voice is either there or it is not there, without the process of building up and cultivating as in the case of the girl, but with the voice there must exist as well the temperament. Boys' voices are very often overworked in church choirs. And with either girl or boy the overworking of the voice should be guarded against as zealously as the overworking of their little bodies.

When a boy's voice changes he is discouraged. He must lay aside all the things that he has learned to sing as he lays aside his baby clothes. Again, the boy thinks of making money or of entering college to acquire a profession. In either instance he refuses to face the position of giving up years to study and preparation for the career of a singer. Many youths have fine voices, but they will not, or very frequently they cannot, take the time to struggle and work things out to a full achievement.

The Girl Gets the Better Opportunity. In the fairly comfortable home, while she is given musical educational advantages, the boy goes out to begin to earn a living. Again, with the girl, the breaking of the voice is an unknown thing. She has not this discouragement to contend against; she simply goes on building uninterruptedly upon that which she has gained.

American Men Have Fine Voices, but they do not give the time to a cultivation of them; they not infrequently desire to get rich quickly. Of late years, with singing an art as well as a science, with the demands mental as well as vocal, and a scarcity of well-equipped singers, the inducements to men to enter the profession are proportionately greater.

As singers, men may gain both fame and fortune in a briefer time than in either medicine or the law; but they must be willing to devote themselves as completely to preparation in their art as they would in either of the latter professions, and prove as determined in the struggle as they would have to be in the years of waiting for clients or patients.

Certain Points Must Enter into Consideration at the Very Outset, no matter what the vocal gifts may be, and these will go to determine positively the choice of singing as a profession.

It is not everyone that can be taught to sing, even granting an exceptional gift of voice. To become a singer is impossible if you have no ear, for no mathematical combination will put that into you. Time and rhythm cannot be taught; if you do not possess them as natural gifts you cannot acquire them; they are things to be developed, not learned.

Good physique is absolutely necessary to the singer; a great singer is, of necessity, strong bodily. A nervous person should not attempt to become a singer, for here, again, is an insurmountable handicap. Regular digestion is absolutely essential to good voice, and a repeated course of medicine to stimulate it will only add to the intervals of physical inability to sing.

Asking the Advice of Singers as to the possession of voice and talent is of no worth, except as a matter of encouragement. Out of the hundred young singers who may be listened to by an artist, it is quite safe to reckon that only one will take the advice sought. They come for praise, not counsel, and whether the one or the other is given them, keep on pursuing their own way.

If a boy shows aptitude for practice in dentistry, for instance, is he taken the round of dentists of established reputation to settle the matter of his ability? Scarcely. In the natural course of things he is put at it himself to prove whether or not he is fitted for the desired profession.

The first question put by a young singer in these advice-seeking interviews is not unlikely to be, "Shall I study with Madame So-and-so?" naming a teacher of renown. If the answer given is "No," the young singer, having previously made up her mind to the contrary, and being firmly bent on following it, continues undisturbed to put her plans into execution.

The second meeting may be two years later. Again advice is sought; this time to be interrupted with expressions of regret that earlier counsel was not accepted. "I feel that I have lost two years," is perhaps the burden of the plaint. "I think I shall sing for them at this theatre or the other; I should like to make my debut."

"Yes, but you are no more prepared for a debut than I am to give a Greek lesson," will be my answer, and I will counsel her to go to Italy, study quietly, and come out in some small opera house in a role which is suited to her, and for which she is properly prepared.

To ask the impecunious manager of a small Italian opera house to put on an especial opera for a young, unknown, and untried singer would be out of the question. Consequently, the payment named as necessary to carry through the undertaking would have to be regarded as part of the educational outlay.

"But, by this plan," I will say to her at parting, "you will save your nerves; you will save, possibly, a fiasco that might mean complete eclipse, for, singing under another name in a distant part of the world is not at all the risk you would incur by a debut at an important theatre."

After a time will come a third visit, and a third phase of the case. The aspirant has meanwhile sung for one or more managers, and been informed that certain things are needful of accomplishment before she is fully prepared for a metropolitan appearance. Her talent and gifts are recognized, and she is advised, perhaps, to make instead a provincial debut in some other part of the world than Italy. This last bit of advice may be less disagreeable than the prospect of a remote Italian town, which is still farther away from the glitter and excitement of a metropolis.

Time passes and with a fourth visit one learns that study has progressed with a view to prepare, once and for all, for a debut in one of the great centres, a debut that will decide the future finally. "In a week I have an appointment to sing for two managers. I am not very well, indeed I have not felt well for a long time; but I will sing. I have lost so much time; I have wasted two years with the wrong teacher; I must sing!"

The outcome is exactly the one that might be awaited. Any chance of a favorable verdict is overset by the condition of health of the aspirant, and yet another opportunity follows in the wake of its lost predecessors.

So the story continues and repeats itself. Nor is this an example of a single instance, but as it were, a duplicate of many, and by no means overdrawn. And still the question is asked, "What becomes of all the fine voices that begin training for opera, and that never come to a hearing?"

From personal experience the one exception to the ninety-and-nine who have asked advice when at heart, apparently, only a confirmation of their own opinions was desired, was a young singer who needed great courage to follow the course pointed out. This exception should be quoted, and the fact mentioned that for the last three years she has been under engagement at the Berlin Royal Opera.

The voice was of unusual beauty, and had been pronounced by some singers of note as fully ready for a debut. Pleased, but not wholly satisfied with this verdict, she came with the inquiry, "Am I ready to go on the stage?"

The reply was: "You come for my advice, and I give it. You are no more fit to go on the stage than a girl of five."

A simple exercise was handed her, and she was unable to sing it properly.

For a year she studied, and came again. She began to sing *Lohengrin* in French.

"Stop! You have too beautiful a voice to sing like this," was the interruption.

The outcome was that she discontinued her lessons, and for six weeks came daily to me to sing. At the end of that time her voice was quite different. "You have intelligence, you have a voice," was the opinion then given. "If you find a teacher whose ideas are good, you will succeed."

The suggestion was acted upon. She left Paris at once and at the end of six months' study with Signor Graziani, an Italian master, she was engaged for the Berlin Opera. During the period of her appearances there, she studied continuously, by my advice, with Madame Lilli Lehmann.

Out of a hundred, or rather, accurately speaking, out of hundreds, this, to my personal knowledge, was the single case where advice was asked and absolutely taken.

The young girl in question was Miss Geraldine Farrar.

This is not written in a spirit of fault-finding, but with a knowledge of the situation, and of the immense value, to a student of singing, of thought and judgment in every step of the career. It is far easier to advance without the necessity, sometimes fatal, of retracing one's way.

Keep Up Your Self-Confidence; you will need it all. Constant criticism and no praise discourages the sensitive and the ambitious. My one aim in these, and in succeeding suggestions, is to place frankly the result of my own thought and experience, and that which I have learned through observation of some of my distinguished colleagues, with an exact directness that may prove of benefit to all singers.

CHAPTER II

Choice of a Teacher and Where to Study

To know the good qualities of all singing teachers is, for me, impossible, for of late years I have seen few. But this must be said: If a man undertakes the law, medicine, science, he is supposed to understand his profession or he is pronounced a swindler. If a doctor commits malpractice, damages can be obtained. But any man may put up his sign as singing teacher and ruin as many voices as he can, and there is no redress. No examination is necessary to embark on his important calling, nor is there any established standard by which he may be admitted to or debarred from the practice of his alleged profession. No man would pretend to teach the bass drum or any other instrument, without a practical knowledge of it. And yet any man may set himself up as a singing teacher. The singing teacher need not even be able to sing himself, it would seem, judging from frequently existing conditions. But I hold that he must, at least, be able to illustrate what he is trying to teach; he must be practical as well as theoretical.

A great many men can talk quite intelligently on voice production, and yet cannot explain correctly how to produce a single singing note. A voice is seldom completely ruined or permanently injured by self-study. It is only when the so-called voice builders come in that the worst frequently happens.

The Great Question—the Choice of a Teacher—rests upon the intelligence of the pupil. She must know that her improvement is general and well-balanced; not that one or two notes are gained at the expense of the *timbre* of the others.

Pupils should not depend too much upon the teacher, and settle matters with the invariable argument, "My teacher says this or that." Depend upon yourself, try to solve things for yourself. Your teacher may have had a hundred pupils, and not one like you, whose voice may, in certain respects, need totally different treatment to secure its full development.

In the instance of a teacher of reputation, a girl may at once, on that account alone, desire to study with her. On the other hand, the aspirant does not always stop to consider either the method of procedure of the teacher in question, or her own needs. What she should do is to reason, "Has this teacher produced such singers as I wish to be, or such as my class of voice may allow me to be? What is her school? And, above all, what do I require?" Look within yourself.

Every great singer should know just how she is going to take a certain note at a certain place. It may be a something born in her. Take, for example, as illustration, two boys, and give them the identical problem in mathematics. The one will figure it out in his mind instantaneously; the other will add it up more slowly on paper—the result will be the same. The one who has figured it out in his mind instantly cannot tell how he accomplished it, but the one who has worked out the problem more slowly can explain it. The latter will make the better teacher of the two; he not only can do things, but he can make clear his method of doing them.

Not every beautiful singer is able to teach; such an one may frequently be able to accomplish things by intuition, but cannot impart her method of doing them.

The singer of to-day is called upon, and must be able, to figure things out, and to give the explanation, especially if teaching is to be taken up as a profession.

Exercise Your Own Intelligence in Your Study of Singing, as you would exercise it in the study of any science, and through that intelligence endeavor to find out whether the way in which you are being taught is the right one. The pupil must discriminate between proper praise and fulsome praise, because the unscrupulous teacher will commend everything. Listen to your own work with critical ears. The readily influenced praise of friends is no safe criterion. Remember that you have a great public to face, and that that great public will pronounce upon you without favoritism or prejudice. Be your own severest critic.

As to Fads, the great singer, as far as present knowledge is concerned, has yet to be produced whose training was secured by any single one or combination of them. A teacher with a fad is a man with one idea, who stands in the position of a doctor who would cure all ills with a single remedy.

The Teacher Who is Looking Purely for Self-advancement will naturally wish his pupils to appear in public, and will not consider the wisdom of keeping them at their studies instead. On the other hand, the teacher who is conscientious will hold first in mind the necessity of a thorough foundation, and that that foundation is to be a lasting one. *Beware of a Teacher* who gives you music of a degree of difficulty beyond that which you should attempt. After three months or a year of study one cannot sing things that Madame Patti sang in her zenith. Take such music as studies, but not to sing in public. Keep at things well within your grasp, try never to show people what you are incapable of doing.

Frequent Change of Teachers is a serious bar to progress, unless you are able to take what is good from each one and leave the rest. Whether you are capable of doing this is a serious question, which, properly to decide, requires an intelligence ripened by experience; otherwise, in following this course, the outcome will be a smattering of knowledge and an accumulation of faults.

Once you have made your selection of a teacher, give to that teacher a fair trial. You must satisfactorily prove to yourself that his way is the wrong one before you are justified in leaving him.

There is Only One Way to Sing—and that is the right way.

A good teacher is a good teacher wherever found, whether in America, Italy or France is a matter of secondary consequence. Having found a good teacher, a fact which must be proved by your all-round progress, and by the approval of your own intelligence, remain with that teacher until you are thoroughly grounded in your art.

It was my great good fortune to begin correctly, and from the very outset that is most important for the student. For four years I studied voice production with Professor John O'Neill in Boston, and not in a single instance have I had to undo his teaching. I do not think that one of the original class which began with him when I did was with me in the end. He was severe, and many cannot stand four years of fault-finding. His searching criticism, so minute, exacted perfection, ill or well. Nothing escaped him, he permitted no excuse.

An Irish gentleman, he studied the physiology of the voice in his father's library, for his own pleasure. There was no subject, character or episode in musical literature with which he was not thoroughly conversant.

His ideals were the loftiest; he was a man of the highest religious principles and temperament.

My study with him of oratorio was so thorough that when opportunity offered I stepped onto the platform at the Royal Albert Hall in London to sing the *Messiah,* with no other coaching than his.

After three months' study in repertory in Milan, I made my debut in opera. On my first visit to the Maestro San Giovanni there, after he had heard me he exclaimed, "Why don't you sing? You are ready." This I tell as tribute to my professor, and to show that a girl need not go abroad to study when we have such masters at our doors.

The debt that I owe to Professor O'Neill is one which gratitude only can repay. Unfortunately I am not enough of a poet to put into language the depth of my profound feeling.

American Singers Should Not Leave Their Own Country until a thorough foundation in their art is acquired. They should have proved their ability to appear before audiences by singing in church, concert and oratorio. Beyond this the choice of a career, whether concert or opera, should be settled not merely by personal selection, but through a searching test of one's fitness; the separate demands upon these powers are fully treated later under the respective headings of "Concert" and "Opera."

Should Opera Be Decided Upon, there is no better plan than to go to Italy for study and development. But it is of no use to go until you are prepared—which means, that you must have a thorough foundation, and have had the routine of public appearances.

Go to some little Italian town for your debut. Italian is a beautiful language to sing in, and it is both right and proper that a young singer should begin in those operas given there.

By the payment of from one to two or three hundred *lire* you can secure an opportunity to make a debut under the direction of the impresario of the local theatre, and in a suitable opera and role. If you make a success you can continue at the same opera house. If you do not succeed you can make a second attempt in a theatre elsewhere. Meanwhile, you have spared your nerves the tax of the debut in a great city, and you will as well have spared yourself the risk of staking your whole future on a single opportunity. If you make a failure at a remote point, all subsequent prospects are not shut from you by a broadcast publication of the fact. On the other hand, if you make a success it will not be a known event. But that does not matter. You are gaining experience, and you are improving. You can afford to wait for the time in which you may demonstrate results more fully, and in a broader field.

Much Nonsense Has Been Written on this subject and against it by students, but the logic of such appearances is perfectly evident. Would an American impresario get a company together to give a young

German singer a chance to make her debut? I think not. The drawing powers of a young singer amount to nothing; it remains for the public performance to demonstrate whether, and in what degree, the musical powers and stage action justify that appearance at all.

The Test of Singing Before an Audience must remain the important one, a test that no amount of singing at home or in the studio will bring. The opportunity to obtain such a trial becomes as much a legitimate part of the educational expense as paying for lessons, and the money given out for such an opportunity is money well spent.

In many instances a young man on entering a great banking house not only receives no salary, but the parents are obliged to pay for his opportunity. One must pay to learn. The same may be said of all professions, conditions are frequently identical.

For the Study of Oratorio and for Concert, England presents great advantages. The best of artists are to be heard in London during the season, and a wide variety of music is interpreted. Not only that, but one acquires there a proper pronunciation and enunciation of the English language, to which sufficient attention is but rarely given by the teacher.

In Germany, where they have fine concerts, the influence is likewise a broadening one, and in both cases, there is the advantage that foreign travel always brings.

CHAPTER III

How to Study

TIME was when a parent would show off her daughters and announce with pride, even with boastfulness, that they had never had lessons in singing, painting, or in that art for which they may have evinced capability. To-day no one cares to hear singers who have never studied, any more than they would submit to an operation at the hands of a surgeon ignorant of anatomy.

The old Italian operas could be sung acceptably by fresh, flexible voices, so-called natural voices, but the school of to-day demands that one should know what one is doing. Whether we may call it natural or not, we all believe in cultivation. With a baby the natural position of the toes is turned in, but from the time it begins to walk, and in order to get over the ground, that position is reversed, and they are turned out. The school of to-day demands, figuratively speaking, that the toes should be turned out, and turned out as second nature.

In Studying at All Times, Exercise Your Mind as well as your body. It requires the keenest intelligence to become a singer, and without concentration of thought on what one is doing the hope of advance is small.

Pupils May Be Considered as Well-advanced when they are willing to be told of their faults by someone who can point them out. But, from the incapable, one is no more willing to take advice in art than one would be in affairs of business.

Study with Calmness. The painter has his canvas, his colors and the subject before him to depict, but the singer must have everything within herself, and be attuned to do the right thing at the right moment. Consequently it is only through intelligence, through calmness, and through thorough self-command, that the singer can hope to achieve a proper development of her powers.

Singers Too Often Waste Time in Nervous Worry, and in the constant fear that they will not be able to attain to certain ends in a certain time. Nothing can be done in singing within a given time; one can put no limit upon one's self. If, instead of wasting hours in worry, that time be devoted to study with calmness, energy, and intelligence, the desired end will be eventually achieved. If not this year, then it will be in a twelve-month later.

Lack of Self-control: With girl pupils it is frequently the case, particularly at the outset, that they give way to tears, especially at their lessons. Instead, it should be their endeavor to comprehend calmly that which is being taught, unhampered by the fear of being found fault with or of inability to fathom or to understand. Otherwise, not only do they retard their progress, but they spend their money for the privilege of weeping, rather than that of gaining knowledge. No knowledge has yet been acquired by lamenting. Use all your powers of intelligence, and with such a spirit you must in time accomplish that which you set out to do.

No Teacher Has a Right to Ridicule His Pupil. He may, indeed, in order to impress a fault, be required to exaggerate it, and he has very often to point faults out, but he has never a right to ridicule. It is difficult enough for one to rise up and be the cynosure of all eyes without feeling that one may make one's self ridiculous.

Teachers Should Exercise Reason, and teach according to the temperament of the pupil. In the case, for instance, of one who is overanxious, and who is to make a public appearance at a fixed date, the preparation should progress quietly and systematically until near completion, before mention is made of the day set for the event. By this plan preparation will be acquired without the handicap of worry which might go, indeed, completely to defeat it. When the desired end is once accomplished, a self-confidence will have been established through precedent that will work for good in the case of preparation for consequent appearances.

A more phlegmatic pupil may be told plans ahead, and have the gradual preparation marked out in advance without disturbing progress. Exactly the opposite to the first-named example, the pupil of phlegmatic temperament may, indeed, need some such spur to secure the desired result.

There is in my mind another phase, illustrated by the case of a young tenor of pronounced ability who hated his *solfeggi,* and was possessed of a desire to act. The clearest way out of such difficulty would be to allow him to take up a role as if he were to appear in it the following week, and let him act it out. Having once rid himself of his fixed idea he will come back to his *solfeggi.*

Do Not Let a Scale Discourage You, and say you cannot get it. Anyone who works can get a scale, and no one knows how to sing until the scales are done thoroughly and properly. You must be able to sing scales slow, fast and in every way. Do not feel satisfied if you have slipped a bit uncertainly over a few notes, even if the ear of your teacher fails to detect them.

I never to this day start to sing before running through my scales, exactly as the performer upon any instrument has recourse to them in preparation. The singing of scales corresponds to the putting in tune of a stringed instrument. The voice cannot come *near* to being ready— it must be *absolutely* in order.

Vocalises You Can Never Leave. They are the fundamental ground work upon which to build. You can put the embroidery of words on afterwards. And yet there are many singing in opera who cannot sing a scale perfectly, but such fail to reach distinction; they have not arrived, and never will arrive at greatness.

It Is a Mistake to Do Things in Anticipation. The constant dread of not being able to accomplish things exhausts our energies before we come to them, and prevents us from gaining the knowledge necessary to do them when they are actually reached. After we have fully mastered the material of expression, it is time enough to begin to think of expressing ourselves.

Early Discipline is most necessary. One cannot live as one desires; one must learn to give up for the sake of the future, and future advantage. To-day one must be willing to sacrifice pleasure that one may be able to do the work of to-morrow.

A Regular Life is a first necessity of success. The importance of proper diet, exercise and rest has been so frequently dwelt upon as to need no full repetition here, but the fact may well be noted that physical culture, in moderation in its modern form, is as absolute an essential to the development of the singer as it is to the development of the athlete. Each muscle plays its part in singing where there is no other instrument than the body to rely upon.

A Disposition That Will Take Criticism is a requisite. Nothing has ever yet been learned by sulking. If one has not such a character by nature, one can gain it through self-schooling.

The Acquiring of Modern Languages is a most important step in the study of singing as a profession, especially so in the case of those contemplating an operatic career. In the fulfillment to-day of such a career a complete mastery of German, French, and Italian is a necessity. In pronunciation one must be an adept, for inaccuracy in any tongue leads oftentimes to a ridiculous meaning to those versed in it.

The Morning Is the Time in Which One Can Learn Quickest and Best; after taking a rest at midday the afternoon is good for review.

Voice Endurance; if you have not a voice that will stand the exercise of an hour or two in the morning, you had much better give up all idea of becoming a singer, for if the voice will not endure that degree of strain in the beginning, it will certainly not withstand the demands of an operatic career. Rest between the intervals during the morning study when you begin to feel tired, and then start afresh.

The voice is no more delicate than any other organ of the body. The remark was once made to me that the voice was a very slender thread on which to hang a career. My reply was, that life itself was but a slender thread on which to place our dependence. The voice should last as the eyes last, giving way only like the eyes, with the advance of years. When people lose their voices it is through the injury of misuse, just as people impair their eyesight.

Of course those with weak eyes would not choose a profession in which they would have to use them constantly. The parallel of limitation is quite as logically applied to those with weak voices, who would seek an operatic career.

Many seem to consider the voice as a something physically separate and apart, while in reality it is exactly the same as any other organ of the body. Those things which affect the other organs injuriously naturally affect the voice as well; one cannot eat, drink or give way to anything in excess without injury to it, nor can one overtrain. As to the question of voice fatigue, it is unnecessary for anyone to set a limit on the time you should sing; you yourself will know when you have sung enough.

Of course when one feels one's self in splendid condition there is danger of singing to excess, and the practice of forethought and moderation is demanded, otherwise the penalty is paid in consequent fatigue and strain.

An hour daily devoted to study is nothing. There may be teachers who direct an hour's study daily divided into four intervals, a course which will keep pupils with him for a great many years. But the organization that will endure only four quarters of an hour daily must be very delicate indeed, and such should be advised to give up the idea of singing as a profession.

The first act of *Tristan und Isolde* lasts for an hour and a half, and the first act of *Lohengrin* for an hour, during which one must hold almost interminable poses; a test of physical endurance rarely considered in the summing up of general results. The great duet in *Les Huguenots* coming at the end of the performance, requires half-an-hour closely put in. Bodily strength and endurance are the first requisites to support the demand of such ordeals. Without them nothing can be accomplished.

Sing with Ease. In my experience I have met many who repeat certain phrases again and again in a wrong way. Hearing the manner in which these phrases were done I have asked, "Does it not hurt you?"

The reply would be, "Yes, I have a pain in my throat."

"But it must not hurt you there."

"Well," would perhaps be the answer, "I think it is only because I have not sung for a week."

That is a mistake. You may be fatigued in different parts of your body—chest, jaws, diaphragm, but you should sing with ease; otherwise the way in which you are singing is a wrong one.

Take as an instance of legitimate fatigue, a passage in the last act of *Tristan und Isolde:* partly because of the construction and somewhat because of the constrained attitude over Tristan's body, the recurring E and F in this passage keep the jaws open in such a position, to give room and not to cramp the tone, that they become fatigued, a pain that passes momentarily. But pupils should never complain of throatache, as that proves unfailingly that the manner of singing is incorrect.

Work First on Things with English Words, and especially on oratorio. Oratorio is good, too, in that it keeps a religious feeling fresh in the young. Begin with the more simple songs, and gradually increase the degree of difficulty. My own first song was a simple little one: "When We Went a-Maying." Presently I heard something by Mozart sung by one of the girls in the advanced classes, and asked my teacher, Professor O'Neill, if I might not undertake it. Well do I remember the hilarity with which he received the proposition.

Master English Diction: The generally prevailing practice of it is poor; not enough attention is given to our own language. The perfect pronunciation and enunciation of the word, and full knowledge of its value and meaning, are absolutely indispensable. Unless one is capable of mastery in these things, and unless one feels the sentiment and meaning of a poem that one is delivering, it is impossible to convey the full and proper effect of the song to one's hearers.

Singers May Sing in Any Language, even though not familiar with it, but they must know the meaning of each word and where the song takes place. Many sing the "Jewel Song" from *Faust* understanding the general tenor of the text, but fail to know what each individual word means as it presents itself. The familiar "Una Voce Poca Fa" has been brought by singers who wished me to hear them. My question has been, "Do you know what these first four words mean?" And the answer has been, "No."

It is impossible to make any effect upon the public under such conditions; one must know what one is singing about, and have a general knowledge of the meaning if one wishes to produce an intelligent impression upon others.

Arouse Your Own Mentality. Songs with breathing places carefully noted are frequently followed according to direction without a thought on the part of the pupil. Think things out for yourself; exercise your mind as to the reason why. Take up songs without a teacher; develop your own mentality and individuality. You cannot always keep your master by you.

Some Teachers Aim to Keep Their Pupils Always Dependent: such pupils are like old, wrinkled men in the *Kneipe;* they are eternally students.

Have the Ambition to Do Things Accurately. Do not think that you can slip over a certain point unnoticed; it is not a question of being near, but of *having* the note. In every audience there is always one person who will know. Those composing the minority who do know are the people who mould public opinion.

True Advancement. In the very beginning, singers must recognize that their art is a something which they must acquire for themselves. The teacher is an aid, an assistant, but the real work of advancement remains with the pupil. How often a student asserts, "My teacher will do this for me in a year or in a month," as if it depended upon the master alone to accomplish it.

Singing is the most legitimate of arts; no one else can put in a touch with brush or pencil for one—one must face it alone.

CHAPTER IV

Obstacles to Be Met With and How to Overcome Them

SELF-CONSCIOUSNESS may be inborn, and, again, is sometimes instilled and developed by early training. Through constantly being corrected when one is a child, the idea grows that someone is always noticing one's every action, and the question presents itself, "What will people think?" And *that,* even without extraneous encouragement, comes into the artist's life a good deal where every step on the stage has to be considered.

With all singers this self-consciousness becomes more or less a thing to contend with; but to rid one's self of it is the only way by which to gain the freedom of action that is an absolute requirement in public performance.

Too Strict a Training and Constant Fault-finding in calling attention to every little gesture and pose tend to make a girl self-conscious. Under such persistent correction the idea grows that she is being observed when in reality none is paying attention to her. On the stage this self-consciousness, instilled at an early age, becomes a barrier—sometimes insurmountable—to that breadth and freedom of movement indispensable to graceful, untrammeled action.

To be continually arranging draperies and looking to see whether things are properly in position, is a phase of self-consciousness destructive to naturalness. The body must be trained to manage the draperies of itself.

Be Genuine. Instead of doing things with the idea of what people will think, strive to do them rightly, and they *will* be right. Instead of singing from the point of view of what the world will say, study to do things as they should be done. Absorbing regard for what somebody would say leads as well to clap-trap for the sake of appearances, and it is not for mere appearances that we must work, but to have things right and genuine.

It may sometimes be an easy matter to fool ninety-nine out of a hundred in an audience, but there will always be one who is not to be deceived, and upon such depends the establishing of one's reputation. *Lamenting Over Lack of Opportunities* means, oftener than not, a failure to recognize our chances. It is a great thing to distinguish an opportunity when it arises. Make use of the little things. Consider carefully the opportunity when it presents itself and from all points, as to whether it is a good one, before accepting it. Afterward it may not always turn out well, but if such should unfortunately be the case, keep straight ahead. Never go about telling of things that turn out ill. Keep the failures to yourself, for it does not help matters to publish them; if you are able to tell people that you are getting on successfully, it will be of far greater benefit to your career. You may be having a hard time of it, and someone may be jealous of you, but it is enough that you yourself should know these things, without taking others into your confidence.

The more you give way to complaining of such circumstances the more you grow to consider yourself a victim of conspiracy, while in reality no one may be paying any attention to you. Go straight ahead for the main point.

The Chief Obstacle to Attaining Things is the waiting for other people to attain them for one. Supposing one desires an engagement in opera or concert, and one feels that one can properly fulfill it, one should not wait to get a friend to introduce one or to write letters, nor yet expect to get it by singing at people's houses, but go instead direct to the fountain head.

Nothing Is Too Unimportant to Begin With. Of course, I should scarcely recommend anyone to enter the chorus; it overworks the voice to sing with a mass. But if you have a thorough command of your voice and feel that you do not incur this risk, it is the greatest place to see and to learn.

Merit Alone Brings Results. Disagreeable things come up in a career, but the most foolish of people is the girl who asserts, "I might have had the engagement of Miss So-and-so, if I had been as good a friend of the conductor as she happens to be, etc., etc."

When the statement is made that a girl cannot become a great singer without intrigue, that statement is a falsehood. Great singers do not get ahead in that way. They gain their position by their merit, for that alone will the public accept them, and do not for a moment think that it is because of anything else.

No one can do things for one, one must do them for one's self. A singer has only her body and soul with which to face the public; those are the only powers by which results are accomplished for her. *Lack of Pleasing Personal Appearance* is a serious consideration in opera. Supposing one is very short, fat or ugly, nothing less than a phenomenal voice would warrant the undertaking of an operatic career. In concert such conditions would be of less vital importance, and one who has a fine bearing or manner has much in her favor; but manner can be developed. A really inborn graciousness is bound to make itself evident.

Self-control: It is of great benefit to a singer to cultivate an even disposition. If one gets out of temper, the voice is the first thing that suffers. The majority understand what it is to become so angry that one can scarcely speak. How do you suppose one could sing after being in such a state? A great singer does not give way to fits of temper on small provocation, notwithstanding she may have that reputation. She is surrounded by many people, each with his or her especial point of view and each one observant. Some little episode occurs, and through varied description by casual witnesses to it the actual is lost sight of and distorted, or, perhaps, misunderstood through partial knowledge.

In this last aspect an instance is recalled to mind. *Tristan und Isolde* was to be given, and the performance was announced to begin at half-past seven o'clock. When we arrived at the opera house it was discovered that my Elsa costumes had been brought through mistake, instead of those of Isolde. My maid was obliged to hurry back to the hotel for them, while I sat in my dressing-room in a state of nervous anxiety, the hour there, and a great audience in waiting. Just as I reached the stage, and took up my position on the couch, the *Vorspiel* almost over, and the time for the rise of the curtain at hand, the manager came to me.

"How does it happen, Madame Nordica, that you are so late?" he asked. "I am told that it is because you did not wish the performance to begin at half-past seven."

To hear this as a culmination in the final moment, after all my nervous anxiety while waiting in the dressing-room for my costumes, and my mental worry over the delay of the performance!

"Leave my presence! Leave my presence!" I exclaimed.

That was not the time to argue against injustice. Had I said more in such a moment I should not have been able to sing.

He, too, recognized that it was not the time for words, and that silence was wiser. Someone, doubtless, had gone to him to say that spiteful thing, but he should have awaited another opportunity for explanation. If I had given way I could not have sung. This is only a little illustration of how necessary it is to have a curb upon one's self.

A number of people were standing about the stage at the time, and without understanding the matter, or, perhaps hearing what was said, there were those no doubt, who went away to announce that Madame Nordica was in a terrible rage because the manager had made some little remark to her. That is the way the public would learn of it, and in this unfair version it would be generally retailed.

A singer is exposed to hundreds about her in such great companies. In the world at large many people like to represent singers as given to fits of temper. There are ungovernable tempers in every walk of life, but a singer who gives way habitually to temper will not sing for long.

Be Methodical. You cannot study properly without method, and take up one thing this week and another the next; fixity of purpose is a great essential. Nothing must turn you from it. In art everything must be exact.

The Proof of Sincerity Is Application. Many declare their love of music; to teach them is to test the value of their assertion. If you love music, no labor in its cause, it matters not how strenuous, will lessen the ardor of your enthusiasm.

Limited Means are an obstacle, always, but unlimited means are an obstacle as well.

Lack of Tact has never yet made any path the smoother. Very often observers will say, "How can you be bothered? How can you see such uninteresting people? I do not see how you can be so obliging."

It takes just as long to say something rather nasty and disagreeable as it does to say something pleasant, and many times those whom one is least disposed to entertain prove to be people of great understanding and interest.

Occasionally one will find one's self confronted by a bore, and then will come the opportunity to exercise all one's tact in order not to become his victim.

In business it is not possible to say flatly, "I will not do this thing or the other," though one may consider one's services indispensable. There is always a tactful way to settle matters. If a person is inclined to take advantage of one's seeming amiability, one can say what one will or will not do, remembering well that it will not make one more important in the eyes of others.

The Exercise of Tact must embrace the ability to comprehend other people's points of view. For instance, ladies, who are greatly interested in a charity for which they are organizing a benefit, do not see why one cannot come and sing one little song. They fail to realize that it is one's fortune, that one cannot afford to give of it freely, and that one must save one's voice in order to keep it in readiness for legitimate work. Again, they do not understand that invariable consent would mean the devotion of one's whole time to charitable work.

The same people who ask one to sing a song at their house on an evening occasion would be shocked at the idea of asking a jeweler to give them a pearl. The conditions are identical, for in each instance it would be requesting a gift of stock in trade; but this their point of view has prevented them from realizing.

As they do not grasp the actual situation, one must recognize the fact and their point of view, and exercise one's reason. It costs no more to give some true yet perfectly tactful refusal.

Mistaken Vanity. Nothing brings greater discomfort and waste of time than indulging the idea that you are accepted by people merely because of what you can do. Some are interesting because they can dance, others because they are witty, and you, because you can sing. Each one in the world owes his or her attraction for people to a development of some especial gift or talent. To consider yourself an isolated exception is to exercise your vanity instead of your common sense.

Brusqueness comes sometimes from overwrought nerves; one's poor body and brain have endured all they can, and caused one to speak out in a way that one has not really meant. People insist on intruding upon one, arriving perhaps at an inopportune moment, when one is just in from rehearsal, nervous and physically worn out, and there is a momentary lapse of politeness. But one never hears the other side of the case, of the impoliteness to singers. People frequently do not seem to realize either the conditions or the situation.

It is very pleasant to have strangers say, "I have enjoyed this evening," and then pass on; but the people who lie in wait for singers at hotels, and who endeavor to catechize them in curiosity, and with a list of inanities, it is no wonder that they receive sometimes a brusque reply. But brusqueness is, I think, the exception, and while it may sometimes prove a virtue, if it is possible for us to exercise it, silence is a greater one.

The Moment for Study Cannot Wait on Inspiration. Even the best student does not always feel like studying; but one can make one's self do things against inclination. One can give up pleasure and the society of agreeable people, and through determined effort accomplish one's best work. If one wants to achieve a task, one must put one's mind to it and do it, and remember well that concentration can be cultivated.

Waiting for inspiration is many times sheer laziness.

CHAPTER V

Stage Deportment: Either Concert or Opera

*I*NSPIRE *Confidence in Your Audience* on your entrance upon the stage; you want them to feel comfortable, and to convey the impression that you are equally so, though in reality none can be comfortable on coming out in concert or in opera. In such a moment I always feel that I love my public, and that I will do my best for it. Combined with this is respect which the awe of a vast assemblage inspires, and which makes flippancy of manner impossible.

Self-consciousness is difficult to avoid, for one has to remember that one's every look, gesture, and detail of apparel are being criticised by thousands of eyes.

In the matter of confidence, the fact is assured that no one can inspire it who shakes and betrays fright or nervousness. I always feel trepidation in appearing before the public, but I have learned to disguise it that it may not be observed. In a moment like that there is no such thing as being natural; to be so would mean to turn and flee. But one has been taught to walk and to salute a great assemblage, and one must have learned to do both right, instinctively; literally to face the public.

Delsarte's great idea was to know thoroughly in advance what to do to appear natural when under extraordinarily exacting circumstances. *Preparation in Detail Means Command of Resource.* In the moment of stepping upon the stage I do what I have studied beforehand, what I have learned, and what I have observed, for the reason that it is art copying nature. Without a certain set of gestures thoroughly prepared in advance, where would one be? Assuredly not placing one's self in a safe position by relying on the inspiration of the moment. By this I do not mean that one should have a fixed set of gestures, but that the fundamental ones must be well thought out.

An artist at such times must put herself in the place of the person she represents and then act it out. It requires imagination, but to be an artist imagination is a first necessity.

50

One should study before a mirror at every opportunity. It is not a question of vanity, but of forethought in one's deportment for the success of the whole. If one rises from one's seat to walk across the room, the idea is not simply to get there, but *how* to get there—the manner in which one is to rise properly, and move with dignity and ease.

In Concert it is much easier to enter from the back of the stage, and to exit at the side; sidewise the line of the draperies falls more effectively than in turning the back toward the audience. Stand firmly, resting the weight on one foot, changing to the other in such a manner as to avoid observation.

When the head is cool enough to have one's mind absolutely on the undertaking, one is guarding against surprises or anything that may unexpectedly happen, either on the stage or in the audience. One often hears of a catastrophe being averted by the self-control of artists, because, to be in a position to do their own work, they must be in a condition of self-control, and on the alert for the unexpected.

In Oratorio the singer, when not engaged in singing, must learn to sit erect and still, and to make as few movements as possible. At the end of the number never be seated until the conclusion of the postlude, stand quietly to the very end of it, no matter how lengthy.

Personal Appearance is invariably an important item. In dress one should be guided as to appropriate fitness by the occasion. Do not think that on the stage and from a distance things will not be noticed. Everything will be seen; remember that all eyes are upon one, and not only that, but through a magnifying glass as well.

The shoes must invariably be in keeping with the dress, and it is useless to imagine that any draperies, however flowing, will hide them.

Gloves should always be fresh. A woman should be very particular to have her hair neatly arranged; straggling locks impart a general air of untidiness.

Avoid especially anything intricate in dress. Let it, instead, be of a plain, good cut. If it be too elaborate one is prone to wonder whether this or that ribbon is in place; such thoughts detract from one's ease of manner and from one's work.

It is not a question of whether one can afford to have dresses from the most noted dressmakers, but that they should be plain in design and fresh. Do not think "This old dress may be utilized once more, the public will not notice it." The public will notice it. Better a muslin gown and have it fresh.

If anyone points out peculiarities of manner which would militate against one's success, it is always better to listen and to consider the value of the criticism.

Self-restraint in the Song and in the Operatic Role is intimately connected with our stage deportment, and the moment that we cease to command our feelings, in that moment we cease to impress our public.

With a song of deep pathos, as, for instance, "The Dying Child," I have found it necessary to sing it many times, to become, as it were, hardened, so that ultimately I might give an imitation of what I felt. If I did not, my emotions would get the better of me; I could no longer convey a true impression. The outcome would be a breaking of the voice and a failure in interpretation, through excess of feeling. In such case the audience, having received absolutely no artistic impression, and misunderstanding conditions, would say, "She has gone off; she does not sing as she did a year ago."

An instance apropos of the subject is recalled. It occurred during my early career on the final night of an engagement at the Paris Grand Opéra. I was singing in *Faust,* and in the Garden Scene the tears came.

"Aren't you ashamed, Lillian!" exclaimed Mr. Jean de Reszke, who was the Faust of the performance. "Think of your public!"

Commanding myself, I finished the scene dry-eyed, which I could not have done properly had I given way to the emotion so dangerously near mastering me.

Keep your head. You have worked out your part in stage deportment; remember that no one is capable of doing her best at all times, but when she knows her real resource, she comes nearer to expressing it. Inspiration does not always come, but with a thorough self-command, and knowledge of one's powers, the lack of that inspiration at the moment is made easier and less evident.

Repose is Powerful. One should never forget the majesty of the public, and that one can never be too dignified. Take your time; comedy, of course, allows of quick action, but the farther you get away from comedy, in romance and tragedy, the slower the action.

The Revolution in Gesture instituted by Wagner on the operatic stage was fully appreciated by Professor O'Neill, my teacher, and in the days when flippant paragraphs and ridicule were the rule regarding "the music of the future," he was well alive to the truth of the new condition. He often explained to me that the world knew little of these subjects that Wagner had taken up and which would yet be understood.

He asserted that those gods and goddesses that Wagner had created in his music-dramas would bring to the stage a new set of gestures, which could not be used for any other parts. Often since I have thought of the wisdom of his words. One cannot bring those same gestures to bear on any other roles, even in impersonating kings and queens, who are supposed to be past adepts in deportment.

In the old Italian opera very little attention was paid to gesture, and one set served for many roles. I suppose that came in great measure from so much vocalizing, for in numerous operas, as, for instance, *Il Pirata,* the tenor had as many florid passages to sing as the *prima donna.* One cannot vocalize to such extent, and at the same time move about with any freedom, for the simple reason that to do so would mean to grow short of breath.

The Actors' and the Singers' Art: Of course we understand that opera is purely ideal, but the wonder is that there is any semblance of naturalness in it at all, because of the many demands upon a singer. In opera one cannot throw one's self into a role as a violinist throws himself into the performance of a solo on his instrument, for the reason that he has but one thing and the singer has many to remember; neither is it possible in opera to sink one's self as completely in a part as can a purely dramatic impersonator. The opera singer, obliged to count two, three, four and to do things at a given instant, cannot accomplish his achievements with equal freedom.

While the actor need not speak when he comes upon the stage until the spirit moves him, the singer must start with the fall of a baton; it is a case of now or never. The orchestra goes straight ahead, and with the slightest hesitation on the singer's part the situation becomes distressing.

Let me reiterate the importance of accurate study, and how alert every sense must be to catch the exact note at the exact instant and at no other. Add to that, time, the expression of the emotions, and a foreign language; perhaps a complicated costume, with shield, spear, helmet, and wig, and again I say that it is a wonder that there is any semblance of naturalness in opera.

If the player were given a scene from Shakespeare and required to count, and in consequence were limited with an absolute strictness in the time of performance, he would not give so thorough an impersonation. Let, for instance, Madame Bernhardt learn music of the most difficult character to sing to *L'Aiglon,* and it is clearly evident that the demand upon her powers would be greatly increased.

M. Coquelin once tried to convince me that the role of Cyrano is more difficult than that of Tristan, because of the requirement to deliver a certain number of words in a certain time. In opera it is not only required that the words be given in a certain time, but with the accompanying music, marked off by the inexorable beat of the conductor. In a dramatic presentation one may *allow* one's self an instant's relaxing freedom, but in opera that is absolutely denied.

Yet another point, which seldom enters into consideration, is the physical endurance required in opera. It takes great strength of body to lie for the length of time that Brünnhilde does in the last act of *Siegfried,* and then to rise without apparent effort.

The strength to carry out the physical part alone of the Brünnhildes; the courage in climbing to the top of the wings; the weight of shield, helmet, spear and cuirass, until one's shoulders ache, to say nothing of one's lungs—so much is demanded that I wonder that so many accomplish it. And yet if one little slip occurs the house titters. Such trifles one must not mind, but thrust them aside, and go straight ahead. Those who come to criticise trifles are as much beyond the pale as the most ignorant.

The question has been put to me after a performance in which I took part, "But did you hear that awful note that the tenor sang?" And my answer was, "No; but I heard five hundred as beautiful as ever came out of any throat."

CHAPTER VI

Concert

To Avoid Taking Cold When Traveling in America in winter is difficult, for the reason that cars are generally overheated, and constant care is needful to avoid mishap. The only fresh air is from above, and when the ventilators are open the head and shoulders should always be covered with a light silk scarf or wrap. This, at the moment, may seem a small matter to occupy the mind, but if a singer is, for instance, traveling from New York to Cleveland to fulfill an engagement, the fatigue of the journey is in itself quite sufficient without the misfortune of arriving with a cold, which would mean serious handicap.

Do not care what the great "They" think, but put the scarf on and take it off twenty-five times in two hours if necessary. Indifference to casual observers is sometimes a virtue; you are guarding against one of the principal mischances to which a singer is exposed.

Rest After Travel. Supposing you arrive at your destination at noon, and are to sing that evening, it is a wise plan to lie down, even if you are unable to sleep, to relax the nerves and body. Be careful in sleeping, though, not to rest too long, for on awakening with nerves relaxed, it requires some time to get into proper condition to sing.

During the afternoon it is well to wash the face, arms, and shoulders in cold water, and then, in wearing an evening gown, the air will not strike so cold against you.

Before Going to the Concert-Room, practice a little, and if you have a *cadenza,* run through it for ten or fifteen minutes; you must be assured that your voice is in order, and that can best be done before you leave the hotel, for, frequently, the dressing-room being next the audience, every sound is audible to those without.

If there are any steps leading to the stage, mount them very slowly, for to go briskly will make your heart beat and your breath short. Take plenty of time in coming out and plenty of time before the accompanist begins his prelude.

Above All, Have Your Clothes Comfortable; an inch in the waist does not matter to the public, but if your gown is even that degree too tight, the lower ribs and the lungs are cramped, and you need perfect freedom both of lungs and shoulders. A comfortably fitting gown gives, as well, a far easier carriage.

If a new dress is sent in late, and on trying it on you find it a trifle too small, when you begin to sing you will discover the real discomfort of it.

The gown should always touch the floor in front, never a half-inch shorter. That extra half-inch adds to the height and allows a more graceful appearance. Have comfortable shoes and gloves.

Never wear a piece of ribbon, a band, or a necklace tight around the neck if you wish to do your best; check a horse tensely and you get no speed.

Have Neat Music, and never old, ragged pages; let the copies for the accompanist be separate from your own.

Decide Upon the Encore in advance, and lay the notes to one side in your dressing-room, so that you will not be forced to search through a pile of music whilst the audience is applauding.

To Sing Without Notes, if possible, is always preferable, but in doing this you must be very sure of yourself. A concert singer with a large repertory may not always feel sufficient confidence to follow this plan, but in the case of the opera singer it is different.

The Eyes of the Singer mean much to the public, and to fasten the glance on a sheet of music means the complete loss of this forceful effect. In opera one has to look out into the great space where often no one is visible, but the glance of the eye has, nevertheless, its power, and it means invariably the establishing of a current of impression from mind to mind.

In Orchestral Rehearsals for concert it has, from my own point of view, always proved best to sing full voice. It is generally customary to give two selections under such conditions, and it is better to sing them just as one would before the public; one can then better tell what one can really do; the men in the orchestra will understand one more completely, and one will know one's effects with greater assurance. In oratorio, of course, this plan cannot be followed.

The Making of the Recital Program must depend upon your public. Take a metropolis, for instance, where people have the privilege of oratorio and opera, and audiences generally prefer a complete program of songs in different languages. In towns not so situated, the program had better comprise opera and oratorio numbers, and, especially, songs in the vernacular.

In making your programs select contrasts, and do not sing more than one or two sad songs; there is a great difference between the pathetic and the absolutely heartrending. Your hearers have come to be entertained, not harrowed. Above all, do not let your recital last too long.

To begin too early with the pyrotechnics is a mistake, for the succeeding numbers will seem tame after such climax; but lead up to it gradually. Let the closing selections be brilliant, and send your audience home in an exhilarated state of mind, with the feeling that they would like to hear you again.

In the Matter of Encores and responding to them, it is well to distinguish between the applause that is a compliment, and that which means "We want to hear you sing again."

It is unwise to be too prodigal of encores, which should be much simpler than the original numbers, and invariably short. To come forward on recall with a long, elaborate selection to sing is a grave mistake.

In miscellaneous concerts which demand serious work and require generally a grand aria and a *scena,* if encores are permitted select something short and appropriate. One cannot follow a Beethoven aria with "Five o'Clock in the Morning." Consider the dignity of the situation; one cannot descend from it. The singer must always be willing to sacrifice a ringing applause to that which is becoming to the occasion.

The Great Importance of a Good Accompanist is frequently not realized by those in charge of the arrangement of concerts, and singers find themselves proportionately handicapped. It is always wiser, if one has not one's regular accompanist, to send the notes ahead, that the pianist engaged may look them through. To wait until the last moment, and one's arrival on the scene, is neither fair to him nor to one's self.

Lovely songs are often ruined because the singer is preoccupied by thoughts of what the accompanist may do next, instead of being able to forget him completely. But no matter what the provocation, never scowl at the accompanist or betray irritation; it never serves to benefit any unfortunate situation by calling attention to it, and he is doubtless doing the best his powers allow.

To Find a Good Accompanist is so difficult that I wonder that more piano students do not prepare for this career, a career presenting such excellent opportunities, and with so few competent to take advantage of them.

A Singer's Contract very often at her expense favors the manager, but in this matter I am not speaking of those who can command terms. Have your contract looked into by a lawyer or someone who thoroughly understands such documents. People frequently sign without any proper idea of what they are promising. It is always too late when once the contract is signed to come forward and say, "I did not understand this point or that."

Before making an agreement it is well invariably to write out a little memorandum of what one reasonably wants, to rely upon the memory entirely in discussing things is to discover later that some item has been forgotten. Once having signed, keep your word.

Personally I have had little trouble, but through observation I have found that women who earn money in large sums are looked upon as legitimate prey by adventurers. In this respect men are much more fortunate than women, for the reason that they are possessed of a keener business sense. But a woman with a minimum of that keener sense can cultivate it, and the well-spent fee exacted for professional consultation will aid her to arrange phases of business as they should be concluded.

CHAPTER VII

Opera and Its Apprenticeship

*T*HE *Apprenticeship to Grand Opera* comes about gradually, as does the building up of any structure, and begins in a way in concert and oratorio. With the experience of appearing before the public one grows to know one's self, and to discover by degrees what one can consistently endure, both from a nervous, and from a vocal point of view. One has also to prove one's capacity for mastering languages, which will have been discovered long before the completion of the concert and oratorio stage, if one has the love of opera at heart.

Having had some experience in concert and oratorio, being fond of languages, and having studied a number of arias, both in opera and oratorio, comes the question of putting one's powers and aspirations to the test. Unfortunately, in America we have no national opera. We have the lighter comic opera or operetta, but this is far too arduous to be considered as a stepping stone. No young girl, whose final aim is directed toward a grand opera career, can bear the strain of singing nightly in this class of presentation. Again, it is very difficult to alternate with the singing and speaking voice in dialogue and lyrics, and, as is frequently the case, to be called upon to dance, which is death to proper breathing.

If, therefore, one has to go abroad in order to secure a grand opera appearance, there presents itself the momentous question of where to try one's powers. The world's great centers, Berlin, Paris, New York, London, are not schools for the inexperienced.

Considering the Matter by Countries Individually, England, like America, affords no opportunity. Then comes the question, "Shall we go to Paris to study?"

What does Paris offer? Nothing.

In France there are a few smaller theatres where a young singer may appear, but France presents the most difficult of languages in which to sing, a language, which, as they teach it to-day in connection with vocal art, is disastrous to the voice, and one which, I shall put it modestly, not one American in five hundred absolutely conquers.

To proceed with our list, we take Germany, a land with which we associate a presentation of all the classic works; many fine operas which are never given elsewhere, and the masterpieces of Wagner. But in considering a vital phase of the situation, what would a young singer gain by familiarizing herself with a great repertory of operas of which, in America, we know scarcely the names? And it is wonderful what an extended repertory of works, the very names of which are unfamiliar in America, a singer may build up in German cities. As for the operas of Wagner, those are not for babes.

Finally, then, we come to the land of song—Italy. In addition to the performances at the great opera houses in Italy, there are over eighty small towns in which opera is constantly given. The language, compared to French or German, presents far fewer difficulties. The cost of living is not dear, not nearly so expensive as in either France or Germany. Milan, which is the musical centre for students, offers good opportunities; there is a splendid opera at La Scala, and, in the spring, at the Theatre Del Verme, at the Theatre Manzoni, and the Sonzogno.

Italian operas are a commodity the world over, and especially in those centres and countries where opera singers are best paid, New York, London, Nice, Monte Carlo and in South America.

Then we shall decide in favor of Italy. Having reached this conclusion, comes the selection of a teacher there for repertory, a selection in which one must exercise one's own intelligence and judgment; exercising as well that same intelligence and judgment as to whether one is improving.

When I went to Milan to study repertory, two of the greatest masters were resident there, and in full fame, San Giovanni and Lamperti, the elder. San Giovanni, with whom I made my preparation, was a wonderful man, a lyric tenor of note in his day, who came to America with Alboni and Lablache. A remarkable pianist, he could play all operas from memory, and on requirement compose a *cadenza* for any voice as quickly as he could write.

In Preparing for a Debut the conditions are assumed that prior to arrival in Italy the aspirant has had experience in concert and in oratorio. In from three to six months or a year she should have completed a mastery of the language, and have three or four roles sufficiently prepared in which to appear. By this is meant that they should have been memorized from end to end, not only the arias, but the recitatives, cues, and concerted music.

Meanwhile, under a teacher of dramatic action, the roles have been practiced in a large room or hall, until, on both the musical and histrionic side, the singer, not only in the opinion of her master, but, most of all, in her own, is fully ready to face the public.

Where to Sing, and the arranging of the business part of the debut is a question that then presents itself. It is likely that her teacher will know of some competent agent whose business is the selecting of artists and arranging of companies. An impresario in Aqui or some of the smaller cities may be in negotiation with him for singers, with a view to presenting, for instance, *Ernani* or *Faust.*

Well, our student has been at work upon *Rigoletto* and *Traviata;* those are the works in which she feels prepared and wishes to sing.

It may be taken as a foregone conclusion that the impresario is far from being a millionaire. His answer will be, "Very well, I will change my repertory and give the operas in which the student desires to appear, but she must pay me two or three hundred *lire* for the opportunity."

At this the debutante generally feels aggrieved, and that someone is trying to take advantage of her. Her *amour propre* is wounded, that she, who has sung in concert and oratorio, who has achieved some standing in her own country and has for a year been studying in Italy, should be called upon to pay for the privilege of an appearance.

On the other hand, she must consider certain conditions of the situation, and realize, "Here I am, I have never stepped upon the operatic stage in my life; this language is comparatively new to me; everything pertaining to actual operatic experience is new. Why should this man hire a theatre and produce an especial opera for the sake of giving me an opportunity to make a success or a fiasco?"

This point of view grasped, the student is more than likely to reach the conclusion that it is only fair to the impresario, if he provide the theatre, orchestra, artists and music in the desired production, that he should also be remunerated for affording her the trial. I think it must be looked upon as part of the outlay for training; this is not an inexpensive career on which she has started.

By This Plan of Arrangement, the town in which the debut will be made is small; the nerves will not have to be put to the supreme test required in a great opera house, and results will not be exposed to the glare of the world. It takes many years to recover from an unsuccessful appearance at an important opera house. If, in her far away undertaking, success is achieved, the young singer stands a good chance of getting a bonafide offer. If she should make a fiasco, she could not expect to secure an engagement on the strength of a doubtful beginning; in such case she would think it over well as to whether she could afford a second venture.

In the Event of a Repetition of the Experiment, she should, naturally, select another theatre. None can expect to please the world over, and on that first occasion perhaps much was against her. But that initial venture will be either a success or a fiasco, and of the outcome the Italian public will not leave her in doubt for an instant.

If the Public's Verdict Be Adverse, she should be brave enough to face the situation, and seek to find out the reason for it. But never should lack of success be attributed to intrigue; beyond doubt intrigues do exist, but they do not concern the entire public, and the great public can be depended upon always.

The singer should have sufficient courage to root out shortcomings, to find what they are and their remedy, and to start afresh. She must, too, invariably realize that she is a foreigner in a strange land, with strange customs, and these are disadvantages always. But the main point is to keep straight ahead, and recognize no discouragement.

If a Fairly Good Debut Is Achieved, it may be looked upon as satisfactory enough for a beginning. Some other small opera house is to give a season, and the singer proceeds from one to another; never losing sight of her shortcomings, never resting satisfied.

Usually, after these little engagements, there is a return to Milan, where agents are kept well informed of an artist's abilities and progress; they know what she has accomplished, and are *en rapport* with managers, who are constantly on the watch for acceptable singers. If a genuine success has been achieved, engagements will not be lacking.

To Make Real Progress During These Experiences, the aspirant is, of course, always reaching out for new fields, trying other parts, perfecting herself in languages, and ascertaining whether certain of the German, or even of the French roles, are suited to her.

For beginners some of the simpler, and so-called old-fashioned operas, *Puritani, Sonnambula,* and others, are better. The modern operas are far more difficult, because it is much harder to preserve a correct emission in singing the unusual intervals indulged in by the later composers. The *cantabile* style of Donizetti and Bellini is far better for young singers, in that they can preserve a purer tone quality on all notes.

From This Preparatory Point, the singer goes on to opera of the *mezzo-carettere* or middle character, as for instance, *Faust,* and kindred works. Years are required to go through with such a repertory. Then come the real dramatic parts, in *Aïda, L'Africaine, Les Huguenots,* etc.

Naturally this gradual building up to the dramatic roles gives the opportunity to develop the voice and body, as they must be developed, from year to year, in order to gain the endurance and also the strength, and yet preserve intact the sweetness of tone. The fact need scarcely again be touched upon that throughout this curriculum a strict watch should be kept upon the health, and upon the voice, as has been several times mentioned.

The Provisions of Nature Are Toward Protection. As one advances and is inclined to grow a little stouter, all one can do is to take exercise, although this, during a long and busy season, is to any extent impossible. Singers are usually healthy, for that is one of the first requirements; the great amount of oxygen of which they make use tends to expand and develop the body.

With progress in one's career, and when one has a reputation to sustain, the nervous strain becomes increased, and one evidently needs one's nerves covered with fat to shield them. Singers who have banted* or taken medicine to reduce their flesh have more frequently paid for it dearly. One of my colleagues told me that she had banted for six weeks, and could not sing for three months; she had no strength.

Similar instances have come under my notice where the tone quality was affected for months.

Memorize Thoroughly. Do not entertain the thought of depending upon the prompter or conductor. From the very beginning try to be exact in everything you study as to notes, time, rhythm, and text, and learn the role so absolutely that you can sing it either facing toward the public or the back of the stage.

On one occasion, while Mr. Jean de Reszke and I were singing the duet in *Les Huguenots,* I heard a commotion, and turning, saw the

*[Bantingism was a reducing method named for William Banting, a London undertaker who used it.]

prompter close his book, put out his light, and shut down the hood for the night. He evidently felt that he could go home and trust us to safely finish the evening without him.

It is a grave mistake to study with the idea of relying upon prompter and conductor, but no matter how perfectly the role may be learned, one will probably have need of them both. And having accustomed one's self to studying a part so exactly, word and music, will be found of great help when face to face with the intricacies of Wagner.

CHAPTER VIII

Wagner

*I*N *the Study of Wagner* one must begin with the lighter parts, but in his operas the length of a role has nothing to do with its degree of difficulty; to Gutrune he has allotted just as difficult music as to Brünnhilde, the only difference lies in the duration of the terrible strain, which in the latter must be sustained for hours, and in the former for minutes.

Many, without having an idea of their contents or their demand, are imbued with the idea that they would like to sing certain Wagnerian roles. Anton Seidl once told me with great amusement of a young lady who constantly expressed her intention to sing Isolde, when, in fact, she had never been able to conquer the syncopated quartette in *Mefistofele*.

After progressing a little way in the music of Isolde, the singer who is not fully equipped and fitted for the task through gradual musical growth and development, is apt to find the *pons asinorum** of the school boy.

The Unusual Intervals in Wagner are much more difficult for a singer to cope with than those in a so-called melody. The physical part of the singing of his music is more strenuous for the reason that the one great thing in giving it is the attack. By that I do not mean that one should always attack full voice, but *mezza-voce, forte,* whatever the demand may be, and in attack one gets away from the tone production. In these unusual intervals one breaks the current of the tone, which makes it choppy and uneven, and consequently the great difficulty to overcome is the preserving of the color and *legato*.

In ordinary melody or smooth singing, it becomes almost second nature to produce a beautiful tone quality, but to sustain that quality

---

*[*Asses' Bridge:* a critical test of ability imposed upon the inexperienced or ignorant.]

when singing unusual intervals is a great study. Again, for this reason, one must have supreme control of one's voice.

Disregard of Vocal Endurance is common in modern writing, but with all the difficulties to be overcome in Wagner he always gives the singers bars of rest before and after an arduous passage.

In connection with this I may point out a too frequent error, and a grave one, on the part of modern song writers, that in striving for continuous and flowing melody of accompaniment and voice they omit giving bars of rest to the singer. Lately, two young composers submitted to me songs which were very pretty, but one was something like sixty-eight, and the other seventy-two bars of continuous work for the voice. This is not possible, and produces the same effect as a violin solo of continuous tone.

Long ago I learned from Sarasate that it was just as necessary to take breath between the phrases on the violin as it is in singing, as Madame Lablanche put it, "Air between the phrases," and that was something in vocal writing which Wagner understood to perfection.

The longest passage by him of which I know, and that proves an exception in this matter of regard for the singer, is the "Liebestod" in *Tristan und Isolde,* and in it there is not a single bar of rest.

To Sing with a Fixed Do [tonic] is absolutely necessary in the study of Wagner. Take as an instance of the importance of this "Brünnhilde's Immolation," in the last act of *Die Götterdämmerung,* in which there are, I believe, seventeen changes of key and nine of time. If one had to count out the position of the *Do* each time the key changed, one would be at sea; the old-fashioned method of a changeable *Do* would prove of small reliance.

A Knowledge of Reading at Sight, if one has been properly taught, with a fixed *Do,* is of inestimable value in the singing of Wagner. The early training plays a vital part in the delivery of his music in the later career. Without that thorough foundation there can be but one result in attempting Wagnerian roles; and above all, do not neglect to learn to read at sight.

Before Entering Upon the Study of Wagner, to which one must come through gradual and many-sided development, it is well for students to take up a page of his music and experiment as to whether they can sing it in time and tune. I know of a beautiful singer and one possessed of a fine voice, who was put to studying one of the Valkyrie at the Metropolitan and could not learn it; the foundation was lacking.

To Sing Absolutely by Ear is necessary in every Wagnerian opera.

One must not accustom one's self to sing depending upon the conductor, for in Wagner's music, above that of all other composers, one can have no free movement on the stage, with one eye on the director. It is enough to be able to listen.

In concerted music it is needful to depend upon his beat, but in singing music allotted to the solo voice one must be able to deliver it with equal assurance, whether facing him or otherwise, or even when one is out of sight. Again, many times the lights are so dim that both prompter and conductor are invisible.

In many instances one will be very far back on the stage or high up; then one cannot hear so plainly, as sound takes time to travel. In such cases the voice does not reach the audience with exactness unless one anticipates a little, depending upon one's self with an absolute knowledge of the music, free from reliance for help from the conductor.

In Studying a Wagnerian Role, take twenty-five or thirty bars, and review continually, always with the accompaniment. It is necessary that every note of the music be played, and not merely occasional chords, otherwise, when one comes to sing with orchestra, there will be many bars that one has never heard before, and even with this plan of exactness in preparation the full instrumental ensemble brings unfamiliar episodes.

The Proper Study Plan is to devote the morning hours, when one is freshest, to the new, and the afternoon to reviewing. When the first act is learned, little by little, with constant repetition, take up the one following in the same manner; as you proceed, absorb the part, think out all your gestures, and practice them before a mirror that you may discover the best effects.

In All Good Music, Nothing Is Left to Chance; one knows what one is to do, and how one should do it; there is a reason for everything, and one can explain it. Wagner has indicated in completest detail in the score exactly how he wants things sung and acted. But even with these exact directions, it is impossible to tell anyone just how to interpret a role, for that is a something which each must work out individually. One must feel what is required of the personage one is representing, and what that personage would do under the existing conditions.

To Be Familiar with a Role one must be familiar with all the other characterizations that go to make the opera in its entirety; this is a preeminent necessity in the correct appreciation and interpretation of Wagner.

With Proper Vocal Emission everything can be pronounced, even French, which I consider the most difficult language for singers. Attack the hardest points; let nothing rest with the assertion, "It is well enough." Work at that one word which proves particularly difficult, until you have mastered it.

Study the Book Thoroughly, acquaint yourself completely with the subject. A full knowledge of the exact value of the word, according to its application, is of vital importance, for words often vary in meaning in different situations. With Wagner this demand is the greater for the reason that in his librettos, not finding the German vocabulary adequate, he has used coined words of his own.

To sing intelligently is to sing with an intimate understanding of the individual word, and yet many come to me and sing in Italian without knowing how even to pronounce it correctly.

Work for Endurance, for in singing Wagner your powers in this direction must serve as guide. You can very soon tell what you can stand. If there is hoarseness, do not attribute it to cold or to any other cause than poor tone production and overwork.

You can never keep too vigilant an ear for your own voice or consider too carefully what you have solved, that you may come to a just conclusion as to that which you should attempt, and to which your response is equal.

Great Physical Strength Is Required, and long stage training to sustain those attitudes demanded in a Wagnerian performance. The poses of Brünnhilde, for instance, on awakening in *Siegfried;* the manipulation throughout the *Ring des Niebelungen* of her shield, helmet, cuirass, draperies, and spear; the carrying of those up over the rocks and down again, and with a horse that is not infrequently restless and terrified; the fire and smoke in *Die Walküre,* the fumes of which are so hard to keep out of one's throat; the long time that the fire is burning and the intense accompanying heat; these are but a few of the difficulties to be coped with, and to be overcome.

The public fails to realize these things, because of the comparative ease with which, after arduous practice, they can be accomplished.

The greatest of all tests of the endurance, indispensable in a performance, is that of standing on one's feet for three or four hours. Again, endurance is the great thing to enable one to preserve beauty of voice to the end of the opera, and yet allow one to feel that one has not done one's utmost—the reserve power of which one hears so much.

My reason for dwelling on these points is that pupils may have a clearer knowledge of the physical demands of grand opera, of which too often there is an inadequate idea.

In Wagner Everything Must Be Sung. I do not mean that one should slight what is called declamation, but that the tone must always be agreeable, no matter how emphatic or dramatic the requirement.

Wagner Is Not for Young Voices. Young singers do not know how to cope with his music mentally or physically. His works are to be taken up not as the starting, but as the crowning point. Many venture first after ten years of study and experience to reach out for the Wagnerian roles.

People not infrequently say, "We must thank Wagner for breaking a multitude of young voices." The reason, it seems to me, that such voices are so often injured by his music is this: Ten years ago a young girl joining an opera company was allotted the roles of Donizetti, Bellini, or Rossini, roles well suited to her, and which do not present the difficulties or require the experience of Wagner. Nowadays, an aspirant presents herself at the opera house, and the first part required of her is the Elsa or Elizabeth, because the older works are less in fashion at the present time. The public wants Wagner, the young voices are forced beyond endurance, and, consequently, break. To sing him, both voice and physique must be settled; such conditions constitute the only safe ones for the undertaking of Wagner.

Wagner's Music in Concert, unless the program be a Wagnerian one, is, it seems to me, for the singer an unwise choice. A Wagner concert brings out lovers of his music who understand isolated excerpts, but interpolated in a miscellaneous selection I do not think that Wagnerian vocal numbers achieve the effect that is their due.

Stage Fright in Singing Wagner is less acute than in any other class of operatic presentations. With him the extreme difficulty of that which one has to undertake is such that it requires all one's body and soul to accomplish the task. In order properly to interpret the role, one's every sense is so absorbed that the awful strain of stage fright is, as a natural sequence, relieved.

CHAPTER IX

Singer and Audience

*E*XPERIENCE *Increases Nervousness;* that is but natural. The longer one is on the stage, the more nervous one is apt to grow, for the logical reason that when one has made a reputation one must live up to or beyond it. Allowances are made for beginners, but not for artists of established position.

Some are self-conscious through vanity, and cannot walk without thinking that every eye is watching them. Such a phase of self-consciousness may constitute a factor of stage fright, but it is a phase quite other from the one common to the sincere artist in general.

A singer's whole life is imbued with the thought of what impression she makes upon her hearers; if she makes no impression, then she has no reason to exist. The very desire to do things correctly stimulates self-consciousness. She cannot ignore the results of her performances; her first end and aim is to do things correctly, and to please. She cannot get away from the consideration of self any more than she can from self-preservation.

The efforts of the singer are all within herself; of course, the greater concentration she brings to her work the better, but she cannot escape from the thought of the impression she will make upon her public.

To assert that indifference is a safeguard against stage fright is a false line of reasoning. The moment that indifference asserts itself, and she is not keyed up, results are completely sacrificed.

An Indifferent Person Never Makes a Singer. I do not know of any singer of high attainments who can walk out to meet the gaze of thousands with indifference or freedom from self-consciousness. The audience settles itself down to that awful silence to hear one do one's utmost; there is no extraneous agent, no instrument of mechanical construction to play upon and aid one, only one's body and soul can accomplish it.

If one has attained that degree of indifference that body and soul can face such a spectacle unmoved, if one can look upon one's audience as ninepins, then one will not have stage fright, neither will one have the first element of true artistic ability. *The Impression Upon the Public* is not the only important thing, except to the superficial. The artist's first desire is to perform her duty perfectly. It is not to the majority that the public means so much and art so little, such are the exceptions; it is the opposite. Art comes first, otherwise why do we work and fret that every note may be right? The audience does not know it, but a single note has its influence; if wrongly placed it requires two or three bars to recover equilibrium. We know that when it is done rightly it has the proper effect upon the audience. It is, therefore, impossible to separate the two conditions of the situation, the desire to do our duty perfectly, and through a perfect accomplishment of it to please our hearers. We give the best within ourselves, we lay before our audience that for which we have given our lives.

One often hears of a singer who sings carelessly. I have never yet met one whose endeavor was other than to do her best. The singer's desire is to please in art as in life; the person who has no desire to please lives for self alone.

Every True Artist Is Emotional; I have never seen an exception, and emotion goes to heighten over-anxiety. Without being emotional none will rise above a dead level, although excessive emotion will prevent one from doing one's best. In studying it is possible to give way to the feelings, but never in the public performance.

The Combined Magnetism of the Audience; the gaze alone of three or four thousand; the atmosphere of people, so subtly recognized by the singer; the difficulty of singing to an audience on a rainy day, these are but some of the existing acute conditions to be faced and dominated.

An Audience Is Never Passive; the magnetic current is there. If the audience were passive, would many become demonstrative on the appearance of a person whom they had never before seen? The audience speaks first. An artist has to recover from stage fright before the responsive feeling is established. If the audience is not sympathetic, all the more does she need to do her best.

When Does One Reach Perfect Security in Art? When does an acrobat reach perfect security in pursuing his calling? One can never be sure. That is why a great artist is nervous. One is able to do a thing at a given time, because all conditions are right, but, if those conditions are completely altered, that accomplishment is no more possible in the same degree than would be the sending of a telegram without exact instruments.

Mind and body are taxed to the utmost in the moment of an exacting performance, and for satisfactory results the response of both must be complete. Circumstances may intervene during that performance which make response on the physical side impossible, and, in turn, affect mental conditions.

I recall singing in a presentation in Boston when things were going well, but between acts, after changing my costume, I had a chill; the window in my dressing-room had been left open. Sudden hoarseness was the result. The audience, in ignorance of the cause of it, doubtless thought "She began well, and ended up poorly."

Again, one may begin calm and cool, but the farther one advances in the performance the more nervous one grows. Something comes over one's nerves, but with a great artist the audience does not know it. The sole remedy is concentration of thought on what one is doing, although even with that the brain works so quickly that every thought cannot be controlled. Yet with mental and moral equilibrium, one can cause an audience to think that one is at one's ease.

In facing a great audience the struggle against anxiety, nervousness and stage fright is common to all artists, but as you gain in experience, you will become the more able to command yourself. Your first thought is of perfect duty to your art; you want preeminently to acquit yourself well. Then comes the thought "I can do it, I have done it," and you do.

CHAPTER X

The Making of a Career

*I*T *Is Very Difficult, Almost Impossible, for a Girl to Start Out Alone Upon a Career;* she needs the helpful protection of an older person. I can never tell all that I owe to my mother, so just, so discerning, so thoughtful of my welfare, and of my every interest; and to my father, who made it possible for her to be with me in those earlier years of my musical life. And his letters during our long absence were always instinct with courage. Both proved untiringly and fully their deep sympathy in my undertaking.

My Mother spurred me on by her criticism, for she was a severe critic; she shielded me from everything unpleasant that might distract me from my work. Her devotion to me and to my career meant the sacrifice of home ties, and the very giving up of her life that we might enjoy the privilege of study and travel together. There was on the part of my father the same spirit of complete unselfishness.

She was a wonderful woman, keeping pace with me in my studies, and, at upwards of fifty years of age, mastered French and Italian. She was ambitious, and gratified that ambition with great good sense and judgment. She never made an enemy, and was always ready with a kind and helpful word for everyone. The people at the opera house loved and respected her; she is to-day remembered by my colleagues, who so often speak of her.

Her courage, energy, perseverance, and pride enabled her to meet the greatest discouragements bravely, and guided to a way out of them; and my path in art was a thorny one in its beginnings.

Once she had put her hand to the plough, she never turned back. My advancement and my interests were her constant thought; sacrifice on her part appeared to be a happiness; whether the sky was blue or grey, she kept her brave, bright smile.

Courage and hope were the lights that she held up to me, and a sympathy so deep that there seemed no limit to be set to it. Her complete self-command enabled her to maintain a buoyant cheerfulness that conveyed no hint of the anxiety she was at that moment contending against, and of which I oftener knew only when it was long passed.

My First Glimpse of Wagner was with my mother at Bayreuth, where we had gone from Ems with Mr. Jean and Mr. Edouard de Reszke. In the midst of the presentation I leaned over and whispered, "Mother, I am going to sing here some day."

For fear of disturbing some listener, with that sweet thoughtfulness of hers, she only bowed her head in answer, but she caught my hand and held it closely. That was more eloquent than any words of the faith she had in me, a faith that proved a never-failing source of strength. On my arrival in Paris as a very young girl, looking up at the Grand Opéra as we drove by in the early morning, I said again, "Mother, I am going to sing there some day," and again her quiet response filled me with the strength of an unshakable conviction.

What we went through before that end was gained! But it was her wisdom, her courage, and her sympathy that won for me a way through it all.

Toward the end, when her strength failed more and more, she still held firmly to her post, lying at last on a couch in my dressing-room at the opera. Had she been taken from me suddenly, I could not have survived it. But gradually, one by one, she gave things up, until only my own resource, which she had so bravely strengthened, was left me to rely upon. And at last her beautiful counsels, my surviving mainstay, went out with the life that she had given for me.

That is the love and the devotion that goes to make a career, and which receives no public recognition. In such a life of unselfish, of absolute affection, there is no thought of self, no faintest wish for self-aggrandizement. It was enough that she lived in the success of her child.

When You Are Criticized, ponder dispassionately whether that criticism is just. Should you, after study, feel that it is unjust there is but one course to follow, pass it over. Do not allow such things to discourage you; in the end it is always the public that decides.

You Will Profit by True, Sincere Criticism; it is always wholesome, but personal ridicule is not criticism. To feel that the critics are against you, is a mistake. If the achievement is good and has merit, you will generally find that the critics agree in its recognition.

There Is No Doubt That a Critic's Life Is a Very Arduous One; they have to work at night under the pressure of immense strain, after listening to long performances. One must not feel slighted because every little good point is not recorded. *Learn From Your Colleagues.* Certain points that I have observed in the singing of Madame Patti, Madame Lehmann, Madame Sembrich, in fact all my art associates, and especially M. Plançon, that Prince of Vocalists, I have adopted without question. There are some, however, who prefer the blind course of pursuing their own way, even if it be a wrong one, to profiting by the experience of a colleague. Sometimes I have ventured to such the suggestion, "If you will sing, in this certain way the defective tone that bothers you, the result will be otherwise."

"Do you think so?" would be the rejoinder.

"I know it, for I have tested and proved it," I have answered.

Yet I cannot say that my suggestion, so honestly given, met with acceptance. I did not mean that to follow my idea they must admire my style of singing; the suggestion was made on the basis that I had conquered roles for which they were still striving.

Of this class I recall a sister artist who sang Valentina in *Les Huguenots*, and sang it very beautifully. After the performance I complimented her, and spoke of an emission by which she could get a greater brilliancy on the top notes, which in that role are so especially important.

Her reply was, "I am a mezzo, and cannot get them differently."

"No," was my assertion, "no mezzo could ever sing the Valentina; it requires a soprano. Come to me for half an hour, and I will show you how you can get your effect with the high notes."

Her only answer was a reiteration that she was a mezzo and could not do differently. She left me with the misconception that I had found fault with her voice, when in reality I had only given advice which she stubbornly refused even to investigate.

But if I should happen to ask of Mr. Jean de Reszke, "Why do you take a certain note in this way?" he would at once talk the matter over and enlighten me. Of course, we sang side by side for many years, and our interests were identical. It is, on the one hand, either this identity of interest with the artist or, on the other, a chosen self-isolation that decides whether there will be an interchange of ideas so valuable to the sincere.

The night of my debut at the Paris Grand Opéra, an American bought a box and took a party of friends. Of course, during the performance there was much to criticize. In the midst of it he rose up and said, "Well, I don't know much about it, but she's there! She's there!

She's there!"

That, in a way, is my own conclusion; if anyone is "there" I will listen to what they have to say. If I were not able to get "there" myself, I should lose no time in trying to find out *how* others did get there.

People Who Leave Other Professions to take up that of singing should not be off with the old love before they are on with the new. Assuredly it is a dangerous risk to give up a certainty for something so will-o'-the wisp as singing would seem to be with those who do not come up step by step.

One cannot casually take up the law, medicine or sculpture, no matter what phenomenal gifts one may possess, and make an immediate success; neither can the start be made in the twenties. In the teens one should be well along in the languages, and in the general equipment.

In everything it is the gradual growth that counts; singing in this respect does not differ from any other art or calling. Again, because it is such an arduous profession, and so few "arrive," it is well worth doing.

Before Entering Upon the Career of Singer, look well into its demands and requirements. One cannot deceive one's self so readily as to the equipment necessary in any calling as in that of singing. People make excuses for themselves and for their shortcomings, instead of looking fairly at the truth, and casting aside all flattery. On the other hand friends lack the courage to say frankly, "You will never succeed."

In this plain declaration my one desire is to save men and women from bringing upon themselves terrible disappointments, through lack of thought and judgment. I have seen young men's tears drop on the floor, because it dawned upon them too late that they could not make a success.

To assert, simply on the grounds that one possesses a voice, that one should be a singer, is about as logical as to say that because one possesses brains, one should be a Rothschild.

Look well to the demands and the equipment for a career and that the start be not made too late.

An Allusion to Self-denial is almost unnecessary, so much has been already said upon the subject by almost every singer. Regarding it there can be no two opinions; to make a career many things must be given up for the *one* great thing.

Concerning Stage Jealousy a vast deal has been said and written, but perhaps the real conditions of its inception have received little thought. I do not believe that the majority realize what it is to come out before the public and in its presence then and there compete for one's position.

A painter, in the privacy of his studio, can paint and repaint, and blot out as many times as he sees fit before he finally submits the finished work to the public view.

The writer, like the painter, can achieve his results in the seclusion of his study, and then submit the completed effort by which he wins success.

The singer is obliged to prove her art on sight, as it were. There can be no retouching, no blotting out; she receives the verdict of the public in the very moment of production. It is exactly like any other trial of skill, and with the vanquished the situation is a hard one to sustain stoically. Consequently, singers are keenly sensitive to their position.

With an appreciation of these things it is easier to realize, somewhat, why jealousy is more apparent to the public eye in the case of the singer. Imagine what it is to be in a company where the one receives thunders of applause, and the other comparatively none. The situation is much more difficult than that of two painters whose pictures are ranged side by side in an exhibition. Those pictures may occupy the same position for years, and yet neither artist be aware of the degree of comparison to which the great public subjects his work. He is allowed to dwell in a more satisfactory paradise. With singers, side by side, there is applause or silence; there is no uncertainty in that verdict, and no gainsaying it.

The chorus are merciless in showing their opinion of the principals; the orchestra players are keen critics, and not reticent in expressing their views. Of these facts, the singer, who is between two fires, is always conscious.

It requires years to convince the public, and to command recognition. If one does not achieve to that recognition, one has to keep on thus season after season, knowing that each time hope is deferred, one's chances of winning a success are slimmer. A great voice is a divine gift, but it is given to few to find out the why or wherefore of touching the public.

Of course, there are those who can say, "My talents are limited; I can do few parts, I cannot be a 'star.' I must be satisfied." Happiness comes to them, as it does to such in every walk of life.

One Must Be Ambitious to do one's best, to be "It"; not ambitious for what "They" may say, or ambitious for the accumulation of a fortune, but to secure perfection in art. If one does well, it is recognized, and, in the nature of things, if one becomes very proficient, prosperity is an attendant result. But one should not expect prosperity too soon. When an artist begins to earn money, some portion of it should be regularly set aside; a good future waits upon a provident present. *Have Patience to Wait,* and you will see why you have not the same opportunities that may fall to the lot of others. Strive against concerning your mind with the achievements of your colleagues.

In the End, Merit Will Tell, for eventually, as a rule, merit is appreciated in the eyes of the world.

When hope is at its lowest ebb, something arrives. One cannot avoid a certain feeling of impatience in awaiting the outcome, but that should never affect or control one's work. It is a mysterious thing, in looking back at obstacles, to realize the way in which they have been overcome; it seems like destiny; there is no hit or miss in the great plan.

The Reward of a Singer is beyond my power to describe. Great compensations, quite aside from any material ones, and all that is refined and beautiful, go to constitute her lot. The most delightful people in society, art, science and literature enter into her life. Beyond, and above all, she gives pleasure to thousands as well as to herself, for if the delight of the hearer be great, how much greater must be the delight of the singer who bestows it.

I have heard some people say, "I would not have a child of mine go on the stage, it is not worth it."

If one has the voice that warrants a career, nothing can keep one from the operatic stage; if one has not the voice, nothing can put one there.

Great discipline, from early years, is required of all who would become professional singers, but it is the loveliest life in the world.

THE END